500 PATTERNS

for Woodworking, Laser Cutting, and General Crafting

FULL-SIZE PLANS

FRED ARNDT

FOX CHAPEL
PUBLISHING

500 Patterns for Woodworking, Laser Cutting, and General Crafting is an original work, first published in 2024 by Fox Chapel Publishing Company, Inc. The patterns contained herein are copyrighted by the author. Readers may make copies of these patterns for personal use. The patterns themselves, however, are not to be duplicated for resale or distribution under any circumstances. Any such copying is a violation of copyright law.

ISBN: 978-1-4971-0465-5

The Cataloging-in-Publication Data is on file with the Library of Congress.

Managing Editor: Gretchen Bacon

Acquisitions Editor: Kaylee J. Schofield

Editor: Joseph Borden

Designer: Mike Deppen

Proofreader and indexer: Kelly Umenhofer

Studio photography: Mike Mihalo

Shutterstock.com Images: p. 1: Tony Savino (cherry background); p. 6: John99 (laser cutter), Lost_in_the_Midwest (digital cutter); p. 7: Stanislav Lazarev (CNC machine), petroleum man (dust mask), Photo Melon (safety glasses); p. 8: Tony Savino (cherry), Guiyuan Chen (walnut), Pawel Hankus (maple), Evgeniya369 (fabrics), Mayboroda Alexander (vinyl); p. 10: irin-k (tree branches)

To learn more about the other great books from Fox Chapel Publishing, or to find a retailer near you, call toll-free 800-457-9112, send mail to, 903 Square Street, Mount Joy, PA 17552, or visit us at *www.FoxChapelPublishing.com*.

We are always looking for talented authors. To submit an idea, please send a brief inquiry to acquisitions@foxchapelpublishing.com.

Printed in China
First printing

Introduction

I have been designing holiday ornaments since 2014, and I am excited to present 500 of my favorite ornament patterns to you in this book. These designs feature a modern, geometric look that I hope you will enjoy as much as I've enjoyed creating them. My love of art started years ago and runs deep in my family. My father, Wellington Arndt, enjoyed woodworking as a hobby, making and selling his woodcraft pieces at area consignment shops. My brother, David Arndt, is a world-class carver of wood fish and has won a number of international fish-carving competitions.

When I'm creating a design, I like to think about what type of material to make the ornament out of and how it will look on a Christmas tree or as a keepsake that can be displayed year-round. These patterns can be used for a variety of crafts, and the front of the book contains some information to get you started. While I created most of the projects in wood, they really can be used for any craft.

I strive for my works to be pleasing to the eye, combining a clean, refined style with practical functionality. I'm a big fan of Modernism and love the geometric elements that make up modern art. I believe the form and function must be carefully balanced to achieve outstanding design. My goal is to create designs that are new, unique, refined, and sophisticated.

Initially, I designed large pieces of art—metal sculptures and wall art, wood fretworks, inked character illustrations, and home décor—but soon realized that holiday ornaments would offer a larger audience the opportunity to enjoy my artwork. Over the years, I've designed more than 1,000 ornaments, and I continue to create new designs. When I design a new ornament, the first thing I think about is the design itself and what image I want to create. This is one of the most challenging parts of the design process. I want each of my ornaments to tell a story within the design and be pleasing to the eye. Next, I decide what size I want the ornament to be. Typically, I design ornaments that are 3 inches or larger so they can be cut easily and will not be too fragile.

This book contains a wide variety of patterns that offer a challenge for cutting and will produce great-looking final products. I hope you enjoy them.

Frederick P. Arndt

Contents

Introduction 3

Getting Started 6

What Tools Can You Use
to Make These Patterns? 6

Safety 7

Choosing Materials 8

Finishing and Displaying 9

Patterns 10

Holiday Season 11

Winter 44

Stars 62

Hearts and Flowers 67

Fun in the Sun 75

Animals 78

Hobbies 85

Automotive 90

Science Fiction 96

Miscellaneous Shapes and Objects ... 104

Words 146

Index 150

About the Author 152

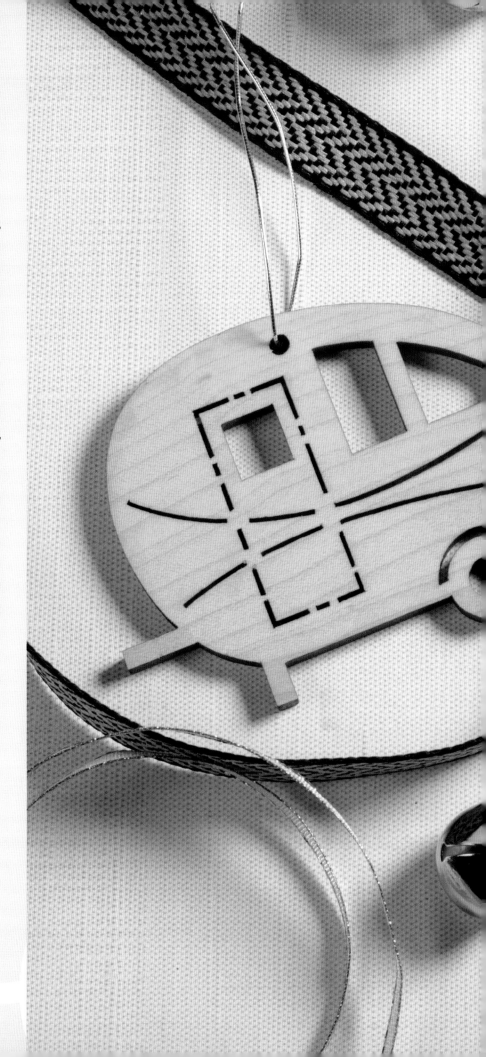

15

39

64

67

72

Getting Started

This section is designed to provide a basic overview of crafting holiday ornaments. Whether you are new to crafting or an experienced artisan, the following pages provide essential tools and techniques to create durable and aesthetically pleasing decorations. Let's begin by selecting the right materials and tools for your projects.

What Tools Can You Use to Make These Patterns?

While I like to use a laser cutter or scroll saw to make my ornaments, you can use a variety of tools to make the patterns in this book. Here are just a few to consider:

A laser cutter provides extreme precision in cutting and engraving a variety of materials including wood, acrylic, and metal.

Digital cutting machines precisely cut lightweight materials such as paper and vinyl, perfect for detailed designs and decorative crafts.

- **Scroll saws:** Known for their precision, scroll saws feature a reciprocating blade that moves up and down, allowing for intricate cuts in wood and other materials. Its removable blade can be inserted into a predrilled hole at the center of your project for detailed interior cuts, making it ideal for handling curves, tight corners, and complex patterns.

- **Laser cutters:** For those looking to work with a variety of materials including wood, acrylic, and metal, laser cutters offer unparalleled precision and control. They can achieve clean, precise cuts and beautiful engravings, perfect for adding detailed artistic touches to any ornament.

- **Digital cutting machines:** Machines like the Cricut or Silhouette Cameo are excellent for handling lighter materials such as paper, vinyl, and thin wood veneers. These tools are superb for crafting detailed and delicate designs with ease, thanks to their fine cutting capabilities.

- **CNC machines:** If you're interested in creating more robust and three-dimensional designs, CNC machines are your best bet. They can carve intricate patterns into wood, plastics, and metals, expanding the creative possibilities of your projects.

A scroll saw uses a fine, reciprocating blade to make intricate cuts in wood, ideal for detailed craft projects and interior cutouts.

A CNC machine uses a router bit to carve detailed designs into a variety of materials.

Protect Your Lungs

Working with various materials like wood can expose you to dust that is considered carcinogenic. Such dust may contain harmful chemicals, bacteria, mold, and fungi, leading to health issues such as eye, nose, and throat irritation; dermatitis; and respiratory problems, including decreased lung capacity and allergic reactions. It's crucial to wear personal protective equipment and research the toxicity of materials, especially exotic types, before starting any project.

Each of these tools offers unique advantages depending on the material and the complexity of the design you plan to create. Remember, the key to successful crafting is to go slow, enjoy the process, and let the tool do the hard work while you guide the design.

Safety

No matter what craft you prefer, take the time to properly prepare your workspace so that your crafting experience is safe and enjoyable. Work in a well-ventilated space and surround your setup with good, even overhead lighting. If you are working with wood, wear a dust mask (either disposable or washable) and safety goggles. If you're working with power tools of any kind, it's always a good idea to tie up long hair, and secure loose clothing and accessories before beginning a project. Take the time to learn any machinery you are using and take the proper precautions.

Always wear the proper protective equipment when working with your scroll saw or when sanding. Dust masks and protective eyewear are essential.

Choosing Materials

Because the projects in this book are meant to be hung on a tree, I recommend choosing materials that are relatively light. Each material listed in this section brings its own unique qualities to your projects, allowing for a broad range of artistic expression.

- **Wood:** When working with wood, I usually use wood between 1⁄16" (2mm) and 3⁄8" (10mm) thick. The ornaments shown in this book were cut from 3⁄16" (5mm)-thick pieces of cherry, walnut, and maple plywood. If you choose to increase the pattern size to make a wall plaque or trivet, omit the hanging point and adjust the wood's thickness accordingly.

Cherry, walnut, and maple were used to make the projects pictured in this book.

- **Paper, fabrics, and cardstock:** Ideal for digital cutting machines, these materials are perfect for lightweight, intricate designs that add a festive touch without weighing down branches.

- **Vinyl:** Vinyl is another excellent choice for digital cutting machines, offering durability and flexibility. It's perfect for creating colorful, detailed stickers that can adhere to various surfaces.

- **Acrylics and plastics:** Suitable for laser cutters, acrylic allows for precision cuts and a polished finish. CNC machines can carve detailed designs into various plastics. Both are available in a variety of colors and thicknesses, making them popular choices for ornaments and decorative items.

- **Thin metals:** For those with access to a CNC machine or a laser cutter capable of handling metal, thin metals like aluminum or brass can be transformed into durable and elegant ornaments.

Finishing and Displaying

There are several ways you can finish the projects in this book. If you used wood with a prominent, attractive grain pattern, I recommend a natural finish; if you chose a bland wood, paints or stains may be best. Always read the manufacturer's instructions thoroughly before applying a finish to any project, and work in a well-ventilated area, using disposable gloves and proper respiratory protection. *Note: Be sure to dispose of oil-soaked rags according to the instructions on the package of finish, as they can spontaneously combust.*

STAINS, WASHES, AND PAINTS

Add color to your projects with water-based acrylics or transparent stains, allowing the natural beauty of the material to shine through. These finishes are ideal for wood, but can also be applied to other porous materials.

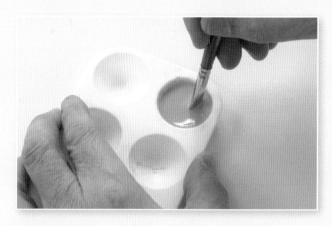

What Is a Wash?

You can create a paint wash by diluting acrylic paint with water until it reaches the consistency of milk. Applying paint in washes allows you more control over the intensity of a color, as you can build up layers gradually. It also allows the woodgrain to show through if you are using wood as your medium.

NATURAL FINISHES:

Oils like Danish and Carnauba wax protect and enhance, offering a hard, water-resistant coating ideal for items handled frequently. These are best for woods or other porous material.

CLEAR FINISHES:

Apply a clear polyurethane or acrylic sealer to provide resistance to chipping and moisture, perfect for items that will be handled or displayed outside.

DISPLAYING

Hang your ornament with a length of decorative ribbon, twine, or a classic ornament hook. Now you're ready to show off your work to family and friends! Keep in mind that all these patterns can be scaled to your preference to create unique designs for any space.

Futuristic Droid;
page 102

Joy, Love, Peace; page 147

Jolly St. Nick; page 35

Scandinavian Bauble;
page 62

PATTERNS

Scan this code to
get downloadable
versions of
the patterns!

Holiday Season 11

Winter 44

Stars 62

Hearts and Flowers 67

Fun in the Sun 75

Animals. 78

Hobbies. 85

Automotive 90

Science Fiction 96

Miscellaneous Shapes
and Objects 104

Words 146

Geometric Christmas Tree and Stars

Delicate Snowflakes

Squares Christmas Tree

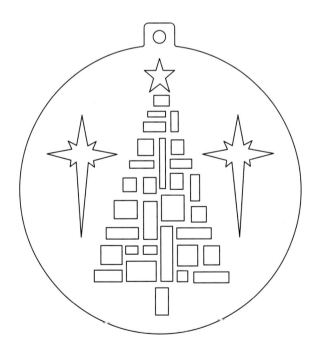

Elegant Christmas Tree

Starry Night

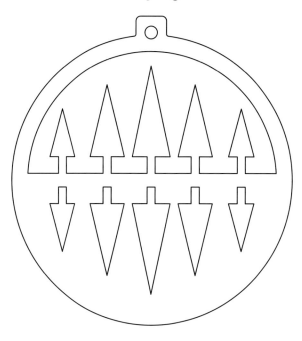

Festive Reindeer

Christmas Tree Lot

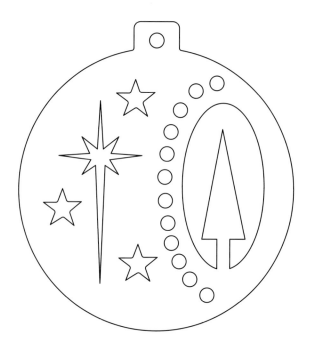

Under the Tree

Trimming the Tree

Light in the East

Snowfall

Santa and Snowflakes

Winter Love

Merry Christmas

Winter Peace

Peace & Unity

Starry Love

Peace on Earth

Christmas Cheer

Let it Snow

Leaping Reindeer

Twinkling Stars

Majestic Reindeer

Bubbly Christmas Tree

Starry Forest

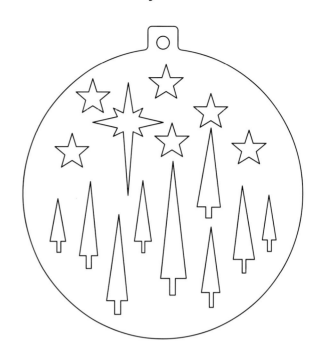

Reindeer Duo

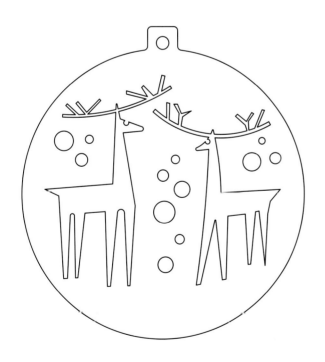

Doe and Fawn

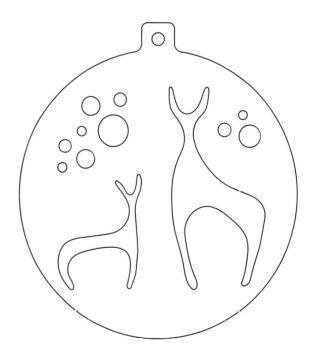

Reindeer Joy

Starry Tree and Snowflake

Patterned Pines

Abstract Holiday

Christmas Tree Lighting

Stylish Diamond

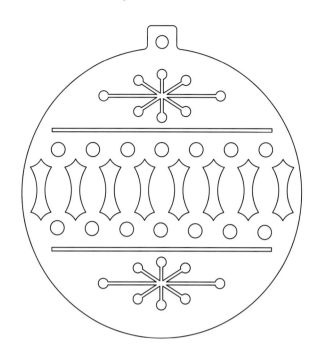

Decorating the Tree

Mid-Century Modern Christmas

Tinsel and Lights

Snowflake Christmas Tree

Forest Gathering

Beachy Holiday

Starry Tree Delight

Miniature Trees

Snowflake Puzzle Tree

Geometric Snow Tree

Snowy Reindeer

Geometric Star Tree

Nativity

Starry Puzzle Trees

Celestial Christmas

Starry Nativity

Geometric Nativity

Hark the Angels

Moonlit Church

Guardian Angels

Wooded Church

Holy Church

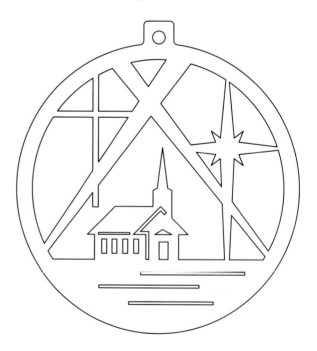

Trinity

Christmas Tree Baubles

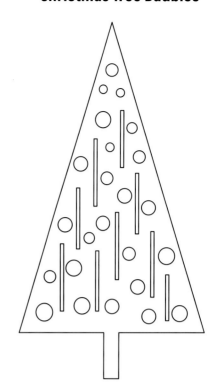

Christmas Tree Baubles 2

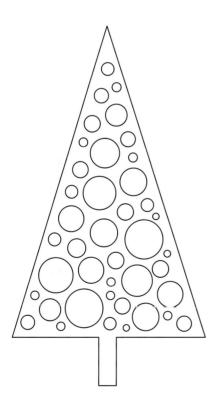

Modern Holiday

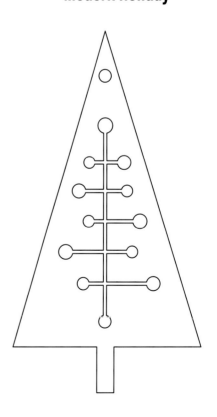

Tumbling Triangles Tree

Starburst

Patterned Tree

Spiny Tree

Oblong Tree

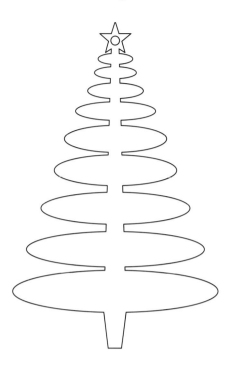

Geometric Jumble Tree

Christmas Love

Diamond Puzzle Tree

String up the Lights

Retro Holiday

Gingerbread Tree

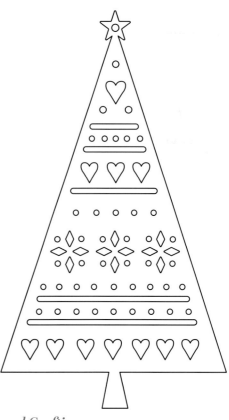

Spiral Tree

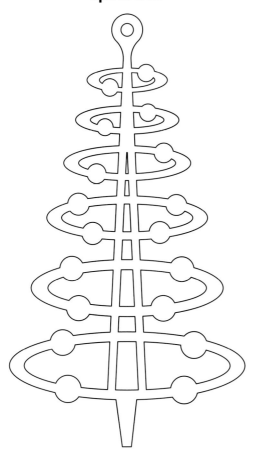

Dazzling Decorations

Holiday Joy

Toy Soldier

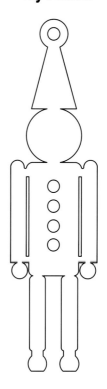

Mid-Century Reindeer

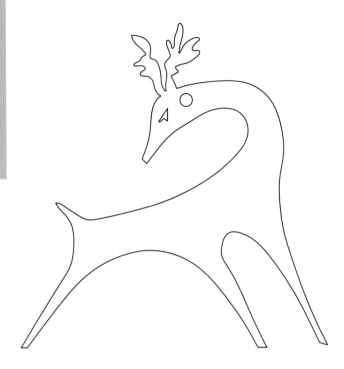

Bubble Tree

Nutcracker

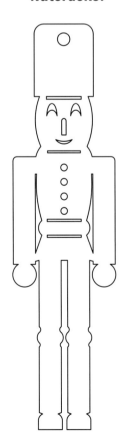

Teardrop Snowflake

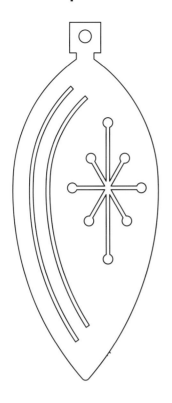

Teardrop Christmas Tree

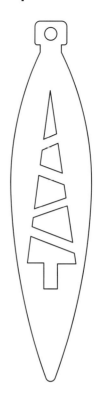

Modern Santa

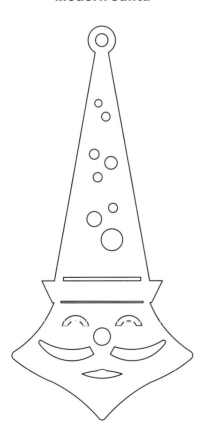

Angled Angel

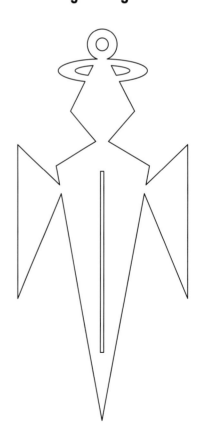

Festive Wreath

Festive Douglas Fir

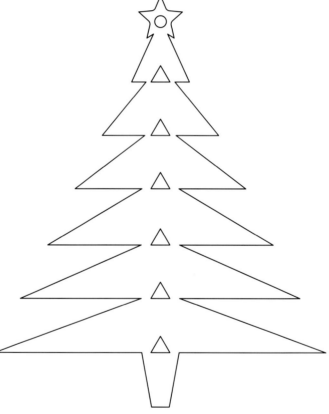

Festive Kris Kringle

Jolly St. Nick

Abstract Santa

Christmas Bulbs and Lights

Father Christmas

Traditional Snowflake

Cheerful Santa

Kris Kringle in a Box

Santa Delivering Presents

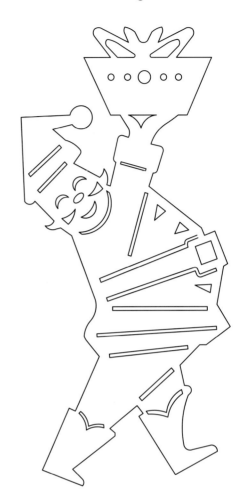

Trio of Trees

Presents Under the Tree

Geometric Santa

Festive Lights

Heralding Angel

In the Manger

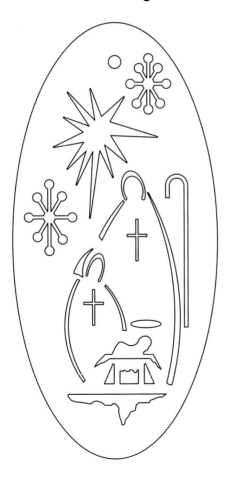

Winter Cross

Christmas Tree Farm

Holiday Travels

Picking Out the Family Tree

Peaceful Drive

Christmas Camping

Christmas Vacation

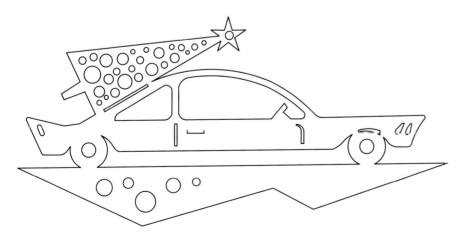

Secluded Sapling

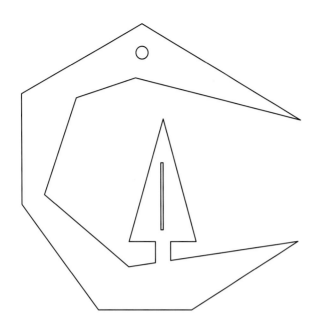

O' Holy Night

New Year Celebrations

Mid-Century Snowflakes

Diamonds and Snowflakes

Stylish Snowflakes

Modern Teardrop Swirl

Festive Finial

Snowflake Teardrop Swirl

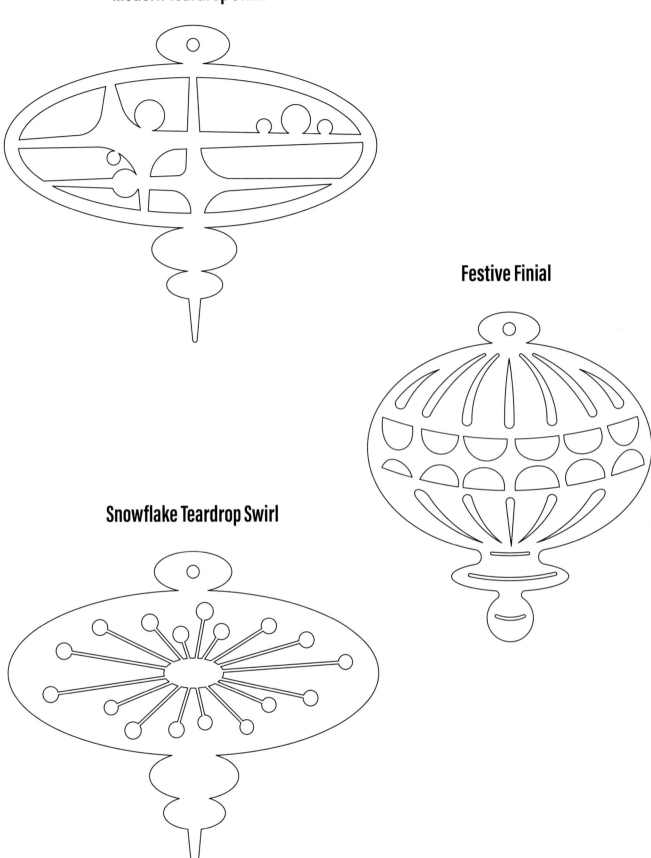

North Star

Happy Hanukkah

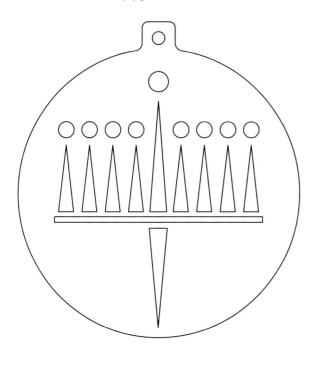

Happy New Year!

Winter Solstice

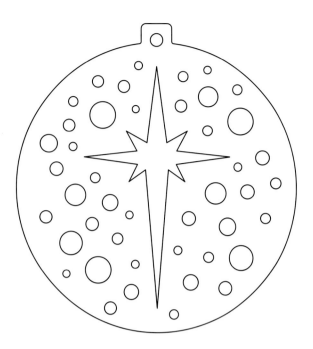

Snowflake Season

Snowy Night

Mid-Century Winter

Argyle Winter

Winter Wonderland

Wintry Nights

Geometric Storm

Bubbly Snowflake

Serene Forest

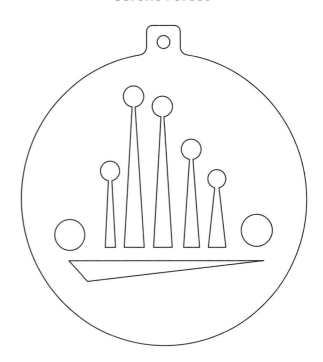

Sweater Weather

Elegant Snowflake

Ultramodern Snowflake

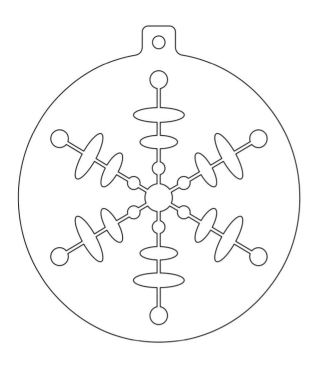

Seasonal Pine Needles

Stargazing

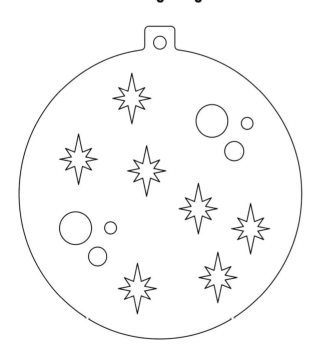

Abstract Forest

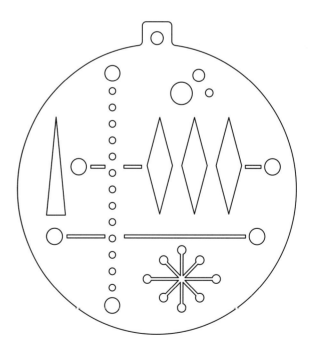

Bustling Blizzard

Nordic Touch

Happy Snowman

Snowflake Finial

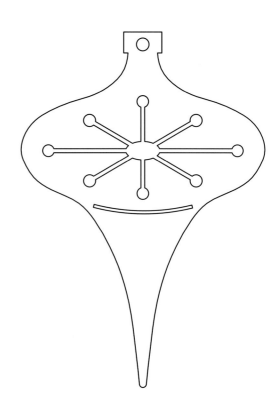

Bubble Snowflake

Light Up the Night Sky

Bundled Up Frosty

Northern Lights

Diamond Snowflake

Lovely Poinsettia

Geometric Snowman

Tranquil Snowfall

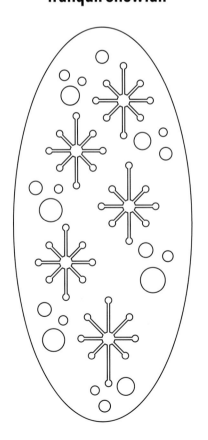

Stylish Icicle

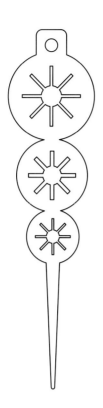

Modern Icicle

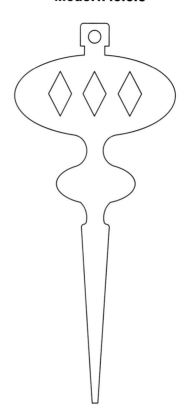

Abstract Icicle

Geometric Icicle

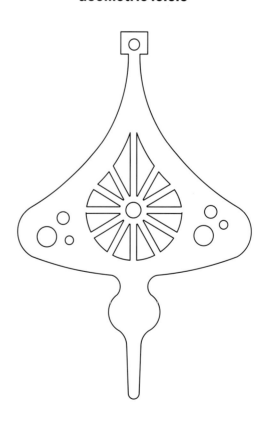

Mid-Century Icicle

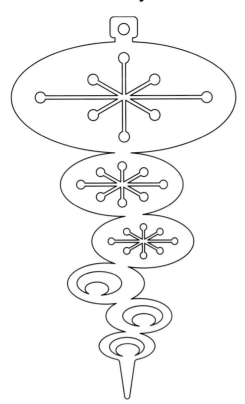

Futuristic Icicle

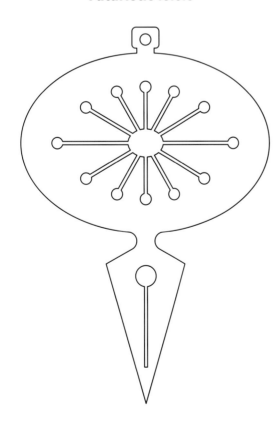

Snowflake Bauble

Freezing Cold

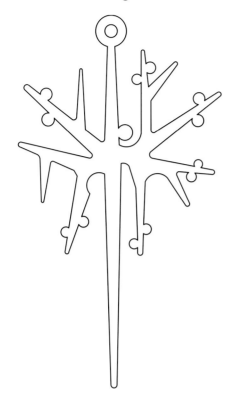

Seasonal Flurry

Snowball Finial

Chilly Winds

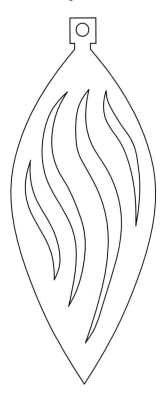

Frosty Trinket

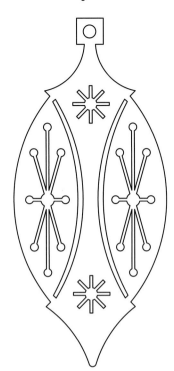

Arctic Morning

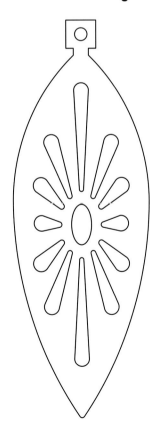

Starry Icicle

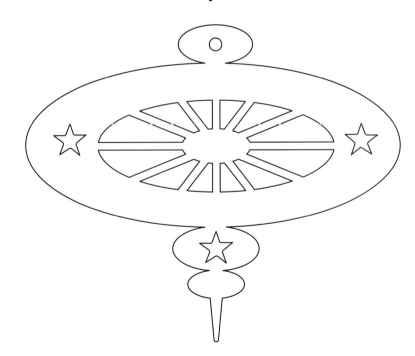

Flurry Fun

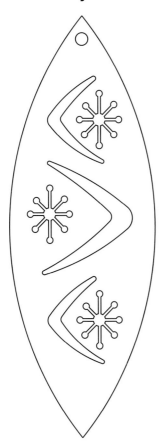

Snow Day

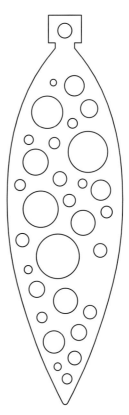

Graceful Snowflakes

Snowball Fight

Chilly Nights

Peppermint Swirl

Ice Storm

Snowbird

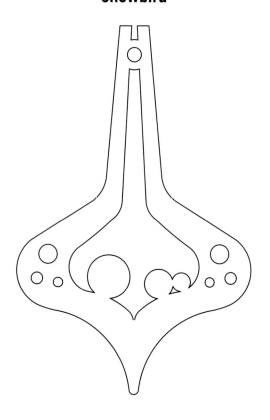

Cozy Sweater Finial

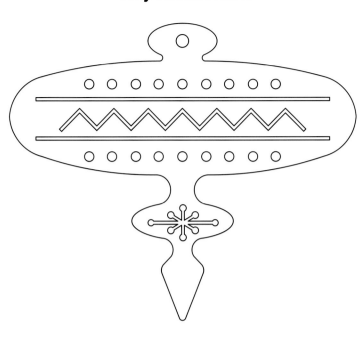

Black Diamond Run

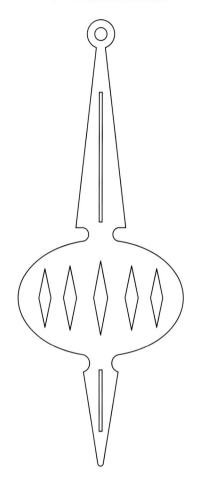

Argyle Snowflake Finial

Wintertime

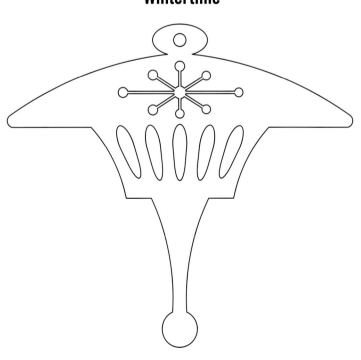

Nordic Spiral

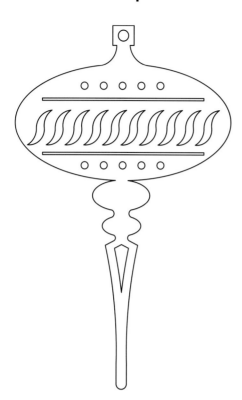

Ultramodern Icicle

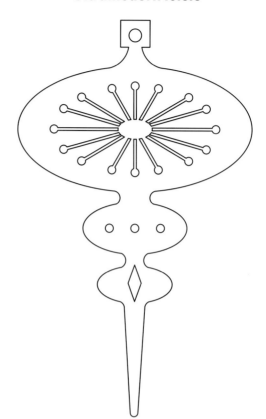

Alpine Icicle

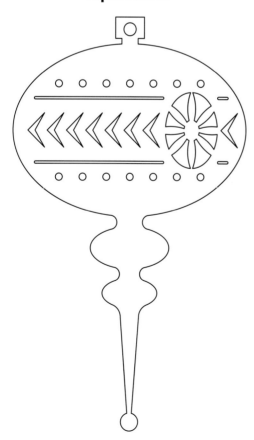

Winter Fever

Unique Snowflake

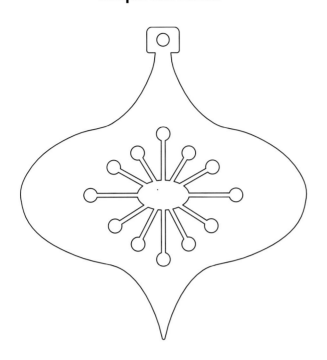

Winter Crystal

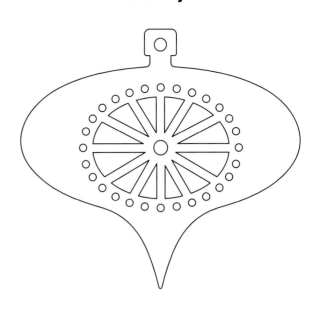

Melting Icicle

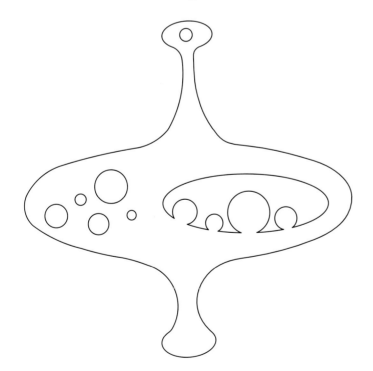

Holiday Bow

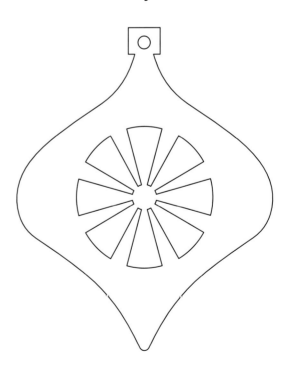

Arctic Knitwear

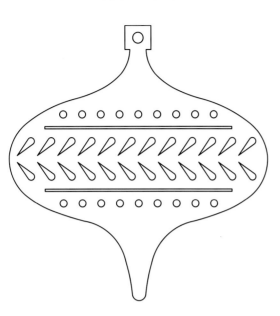

Star of Bethlehem

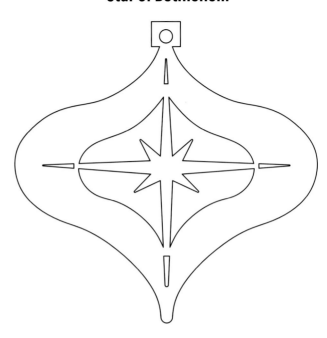

Hailstorm

Scandinavian Bauble

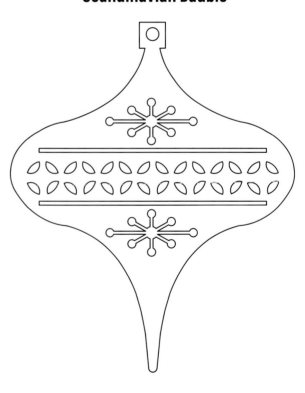

Following the Star

Nighttime Snowfall

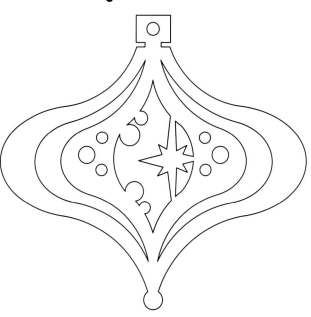

Jingle Bells

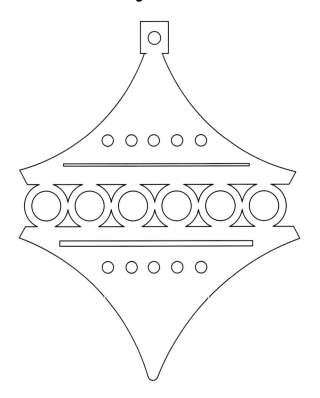

Snow Angels

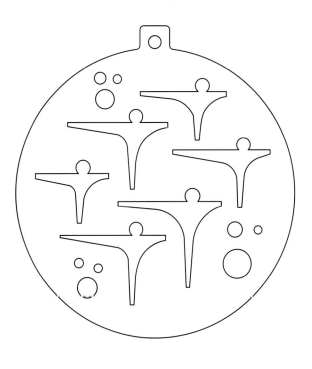

Star Bright

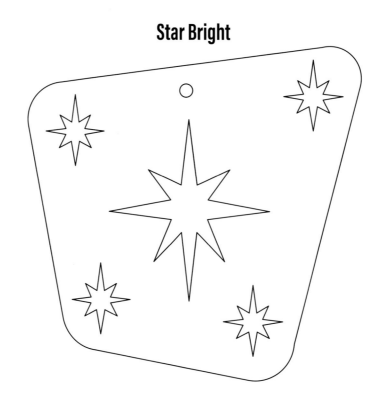

Superstar

Winter Nebula

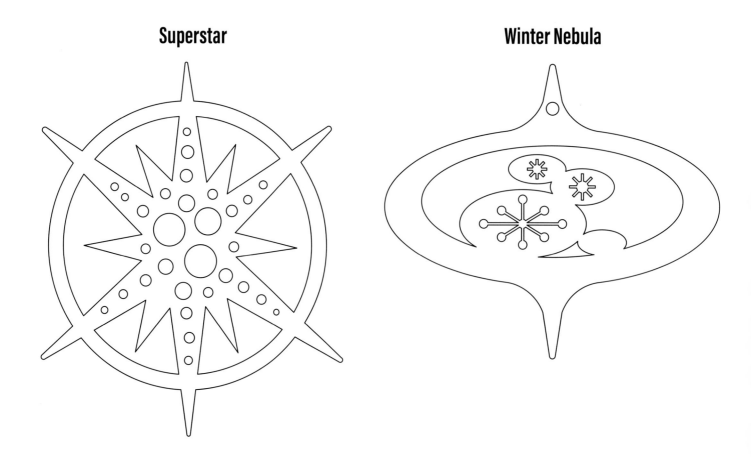

Stardust

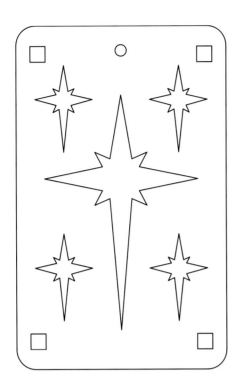

Cosmic Delight

Trinity of Stars

Stellar Light

Supernova

Celestial Trio

Starlight

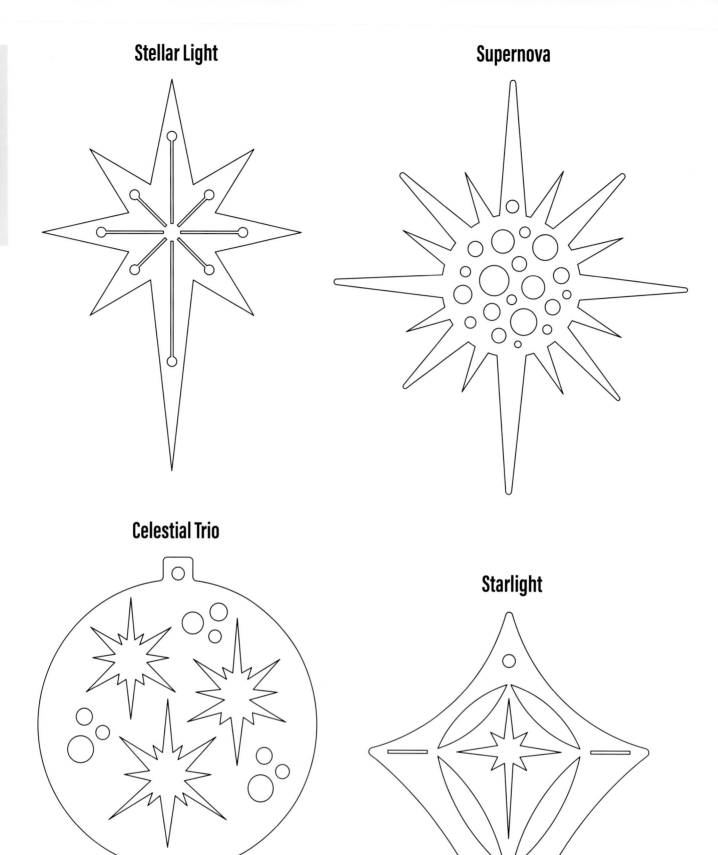

Cluster of Stars

Elegant Luminary

Interstellar

Astral Collection

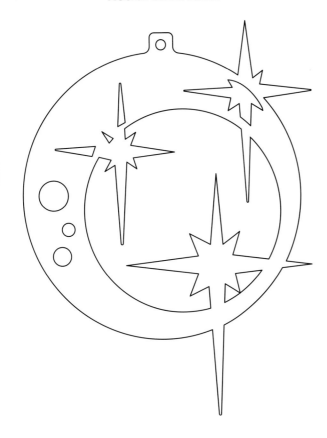

Rising Star

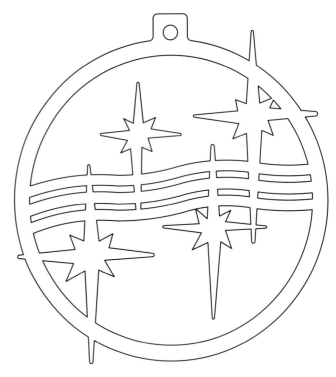

Stylish Galaxy

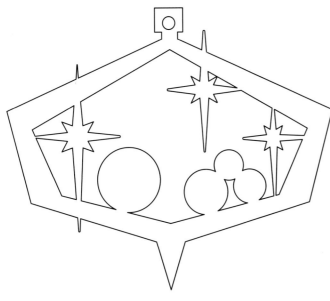

Wholesome Love

Duo of Hearts

An Imprint on Your Heart

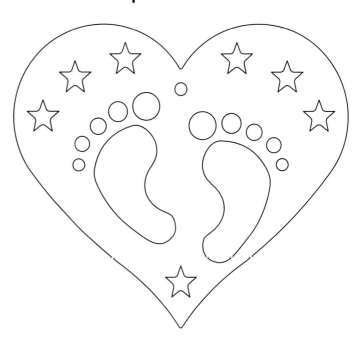

Lovebirds

Heartbeat

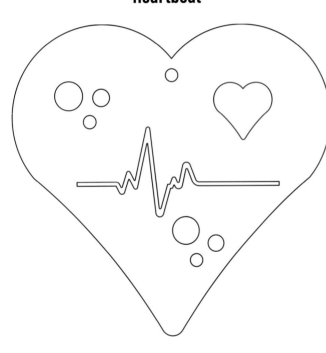

Be My Valentine

Two Turtle Doves

Flower Power

Star-crossed Lovers

Floral Bouquet

Wildflower

Delicate Daisy

Floral Quilt Block

Spring Blossom

Poinsettia in Bloom

Night Garden

Perfect Petals

Fresh Lily

Sunflowers

In Full Bloom

Spring Awakening

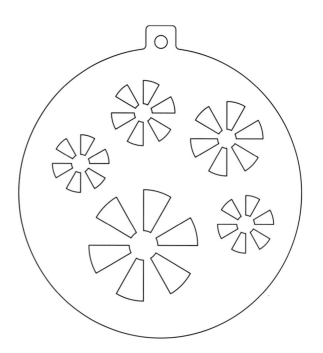

Delightful Dandelions

A Single Rose

Floral Trinity

Dandelion Daze

Blooming Iris

Growing Up

Happy Hour

Sunny Day

Party

Margarita on the Beach

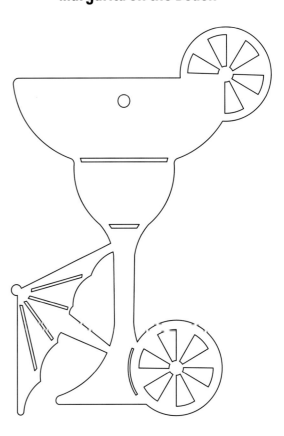

It's Five O'Clock Somewhere

Martini Time

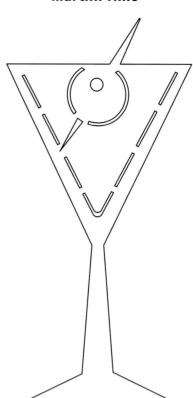

Mixing Drinks

Surf's Up

Hang Ten

Tropical Paradise

R&R

Wine Down

Festive Feline

Kitty Cat

Trio of Kittens

Nocturnal Pets

Purr-fect Place

Something's Fishy

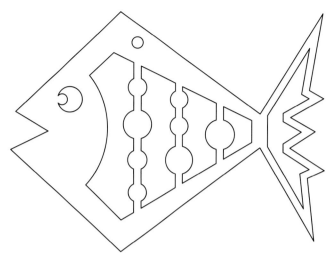

Cat on the Windowsill

Furry Lookout

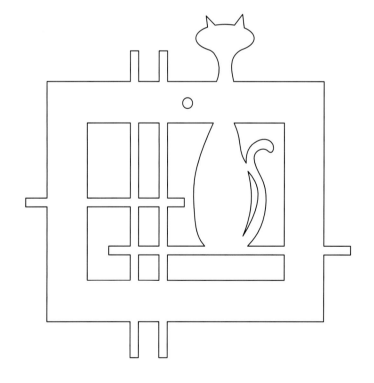

Plenty of Fish

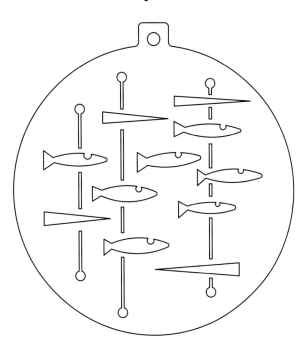

Aquarium Life

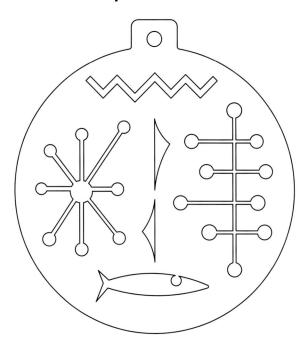

Under the Sea

Swimming Along

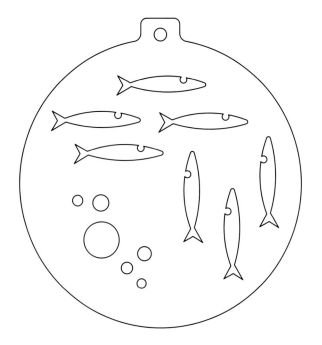

School of Fish

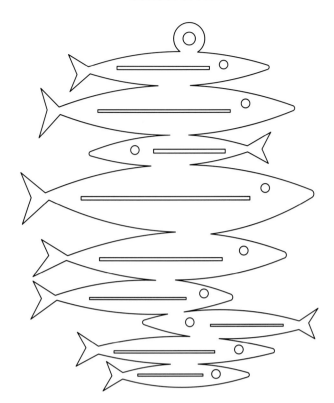

Early Bird

Flying High

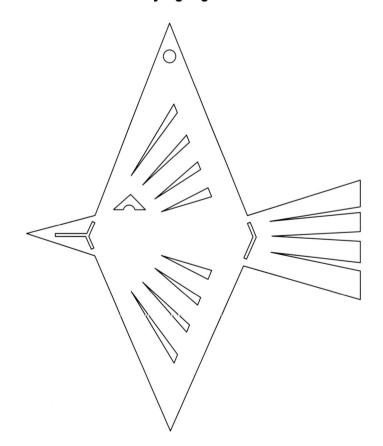

Elegant Cat

Scales and Fins

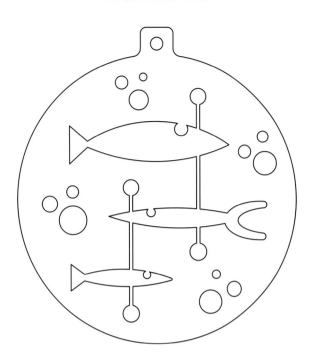

Night Owl

It's a Hoot

Birds of Prey

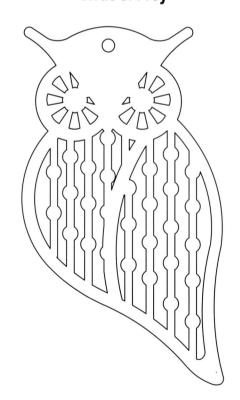

Sharing a Perch

Flock of Flamingoes

Equestrian Love

Buzzing Around

Bee Mine

Squirreling Away

Man's Best Friend

Lion Pride

Music Lover

To a Tee

Palm Springs

All That Jazz

Cycling

Hitting the Slopes

Shooting Hoops

Triathlon

Gone Fishing

Hoisting the Sails

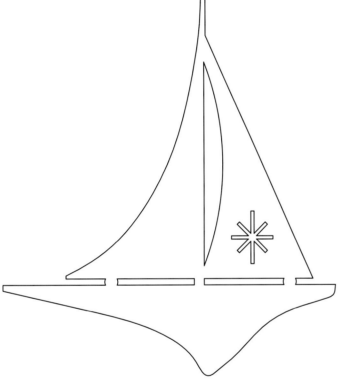

Sailing Away

Nautical Fun

Out on the Water

Sailing the High Seas

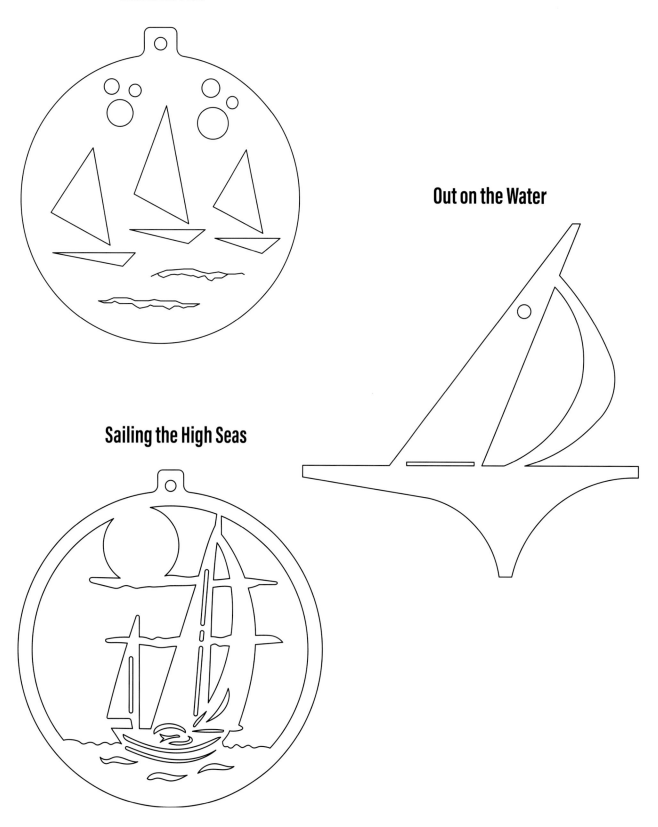

Moonlight Sail

Soccer

Calm Waters

Retro Truck

Classic Cadillac

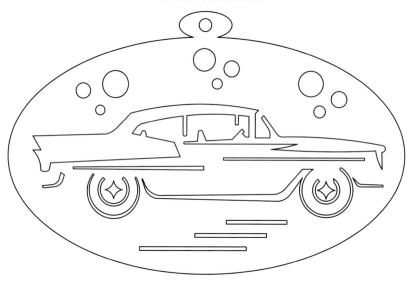

Vintage Car

Sunday Drive

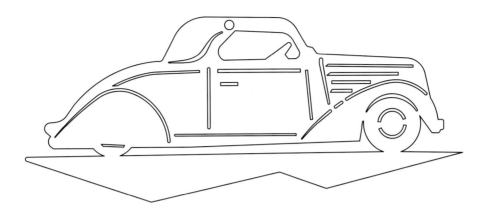

Heading to the Beach

Drag Racing

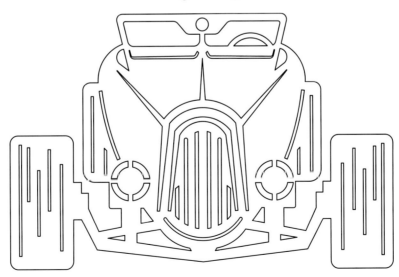

On the Road

Out for a Drive

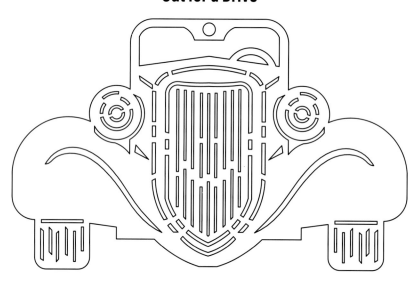

Family Vacation

Speed Racer

Vintage Racecar

Retro Trailer

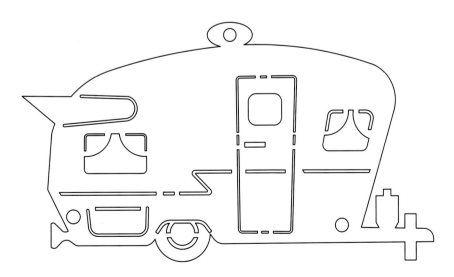

Nostalgic Camper

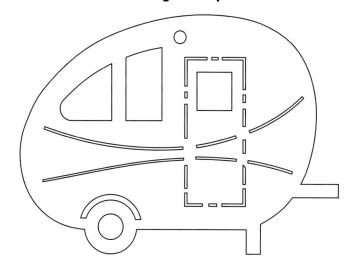

Vacation Motor Home

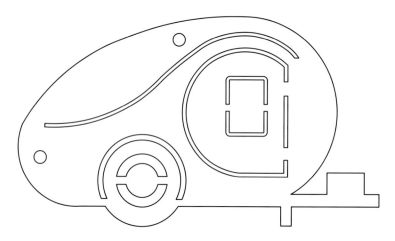

Futuristic Camper

Motorcycle

Tractor

Steam Locomotive

Propeller Plane

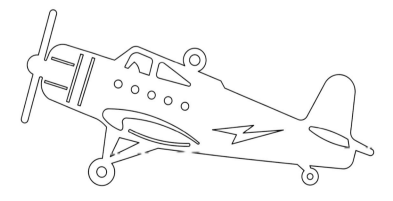

Spaceship

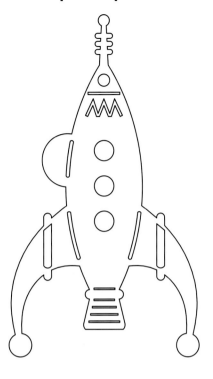

Utopian Metropolis

Alien Ship

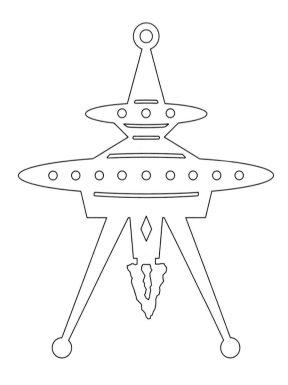

Outer Space

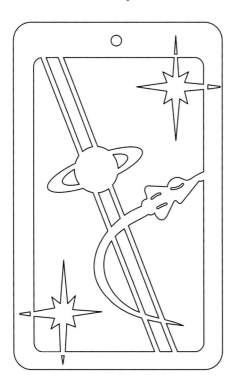

Spacecraft

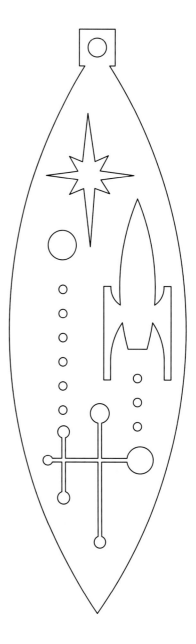

Space Landing

Space Travel

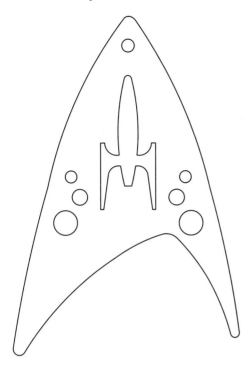

Sci-Fi Television

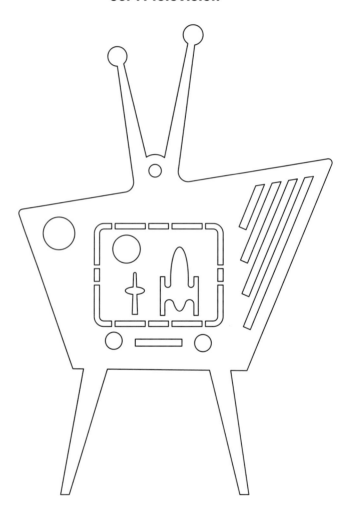

Space Launch

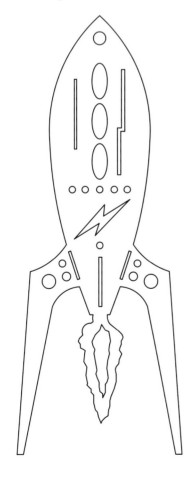

Starship

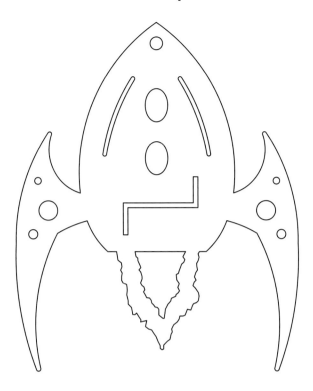

Blast Off!

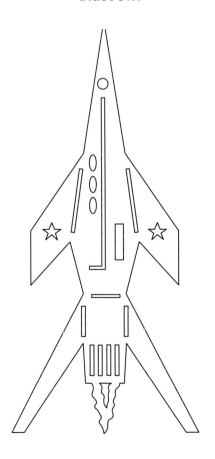

Rocket

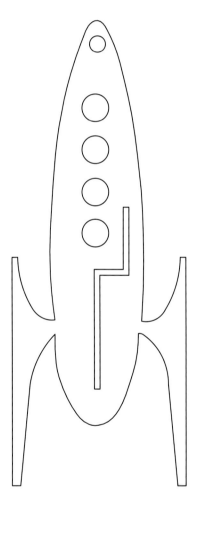

Robot

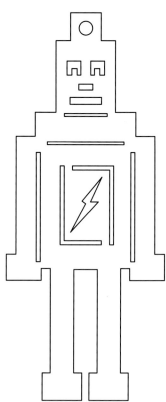

UFO

Futuristic Droid

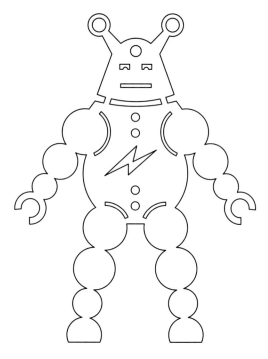

Traveling through Space and Time

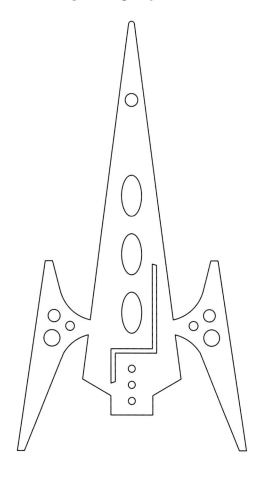

In Orbit

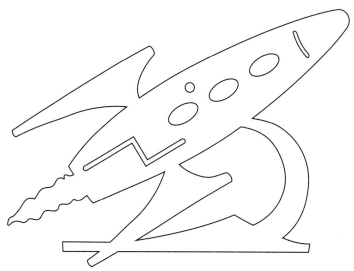

Space Odyssey

Futuristic City

Out of This World

Ultramodern City Finial

Cruising Through the Stars

Futuristic Finial

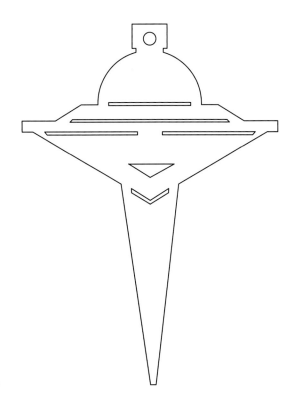

Android Head

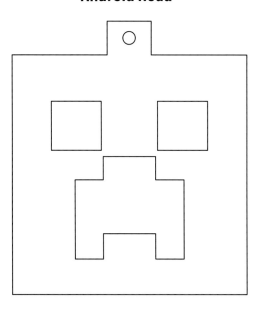

Jukebox

Cosmic Bot

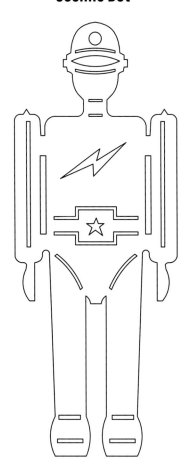

Antique Lantern

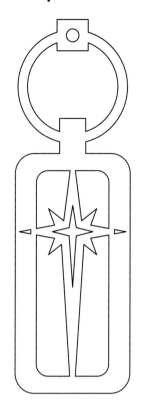

Retro Radio

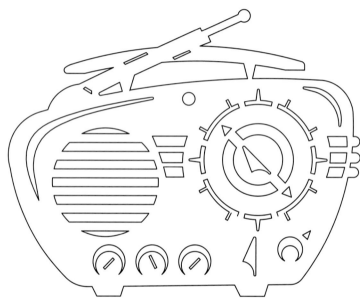

Vintage Alarm Clock

Modern Triangle

Abstract Trinket

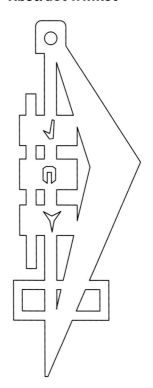

Cat-Eye Sunglasses

Sunburst

Groovy Lava Lamp

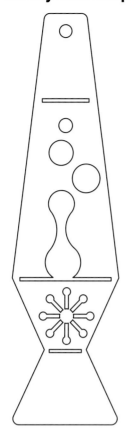

Lunar Bauble

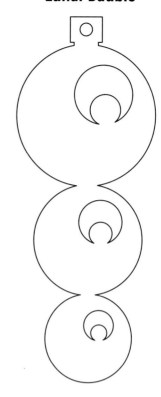

Atomic Snowflake

Retro Television

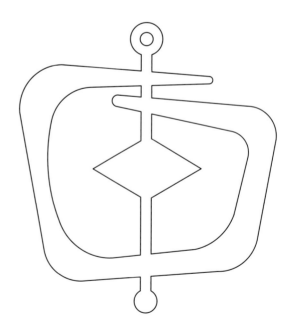

Looking out the Window

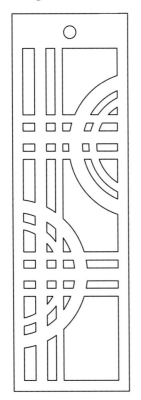

Striped Snowflake

Atom Molecule

Christmas Memories

Mesopotamian Bulb

Melting Bauble

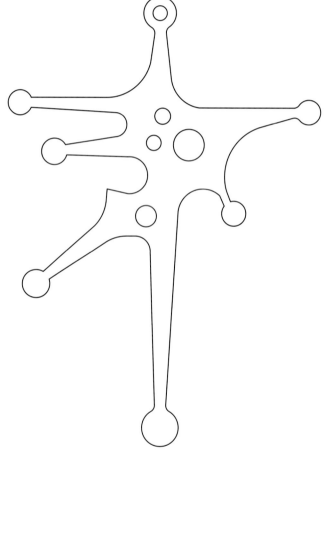

Bubble Trouble

Celestial Finial

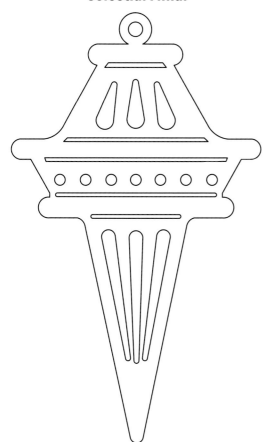

Abstract Bowtie

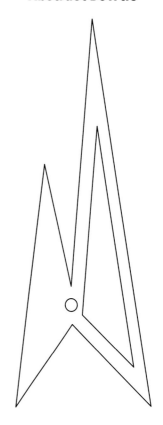

Cheese and Olives

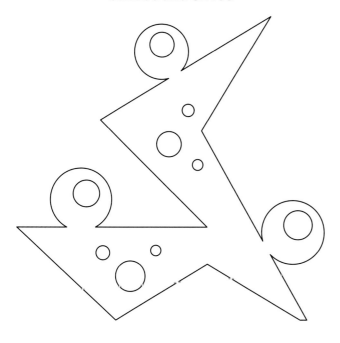

Mid-Century Bauble

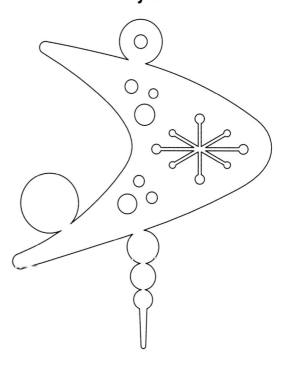

Stack of Olives

Abstract Pendant

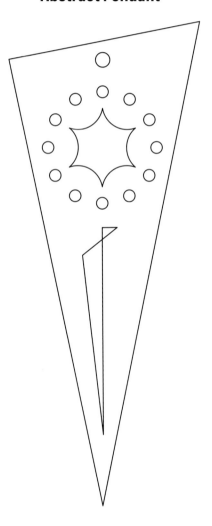

Bubbly Explosion

Pair of Snowflakes

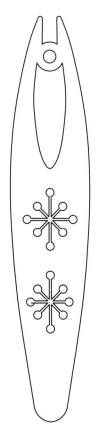

Expanding Bulb

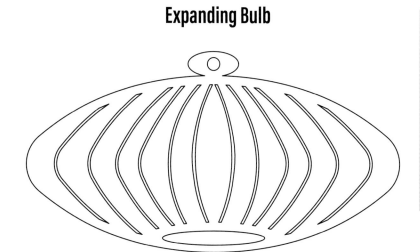

Solar Power

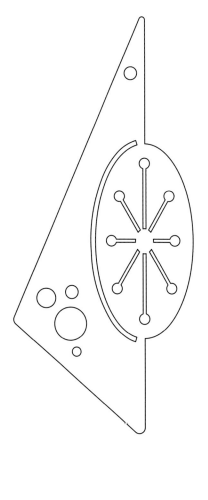

Blowing Bubbles

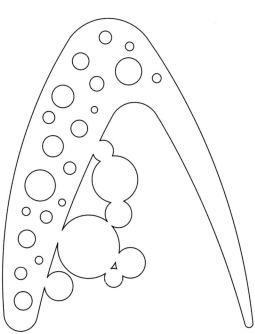

Floating Bubbles

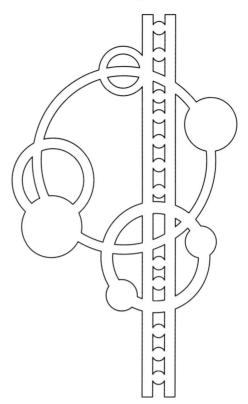

Modern Windowsills

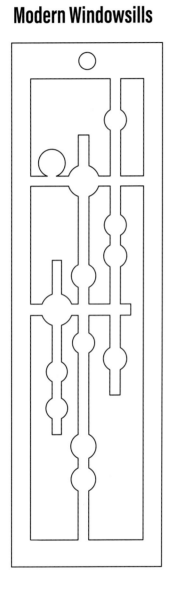

Geometric Diamond

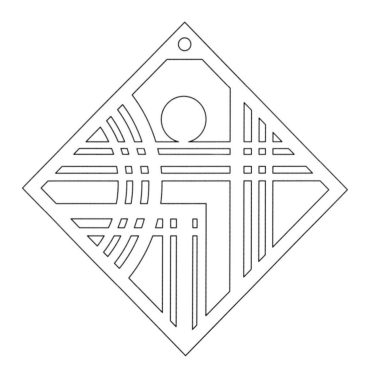

Moon and Stars

Mountain Peak

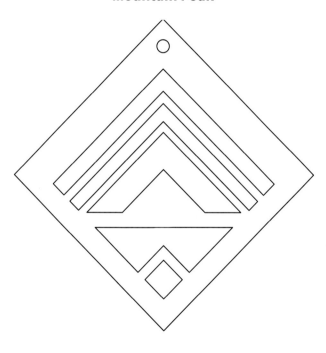

Forest Silhouette

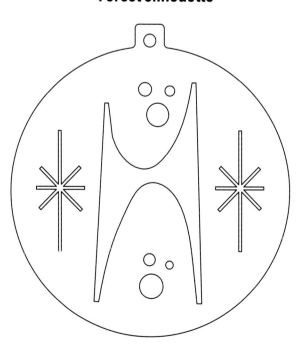

Stacked Ovals

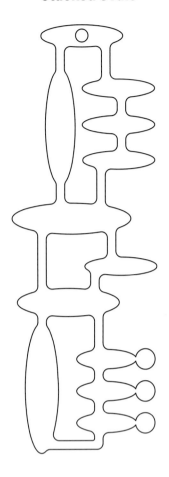

Winter Magic

Dynamic Swirl

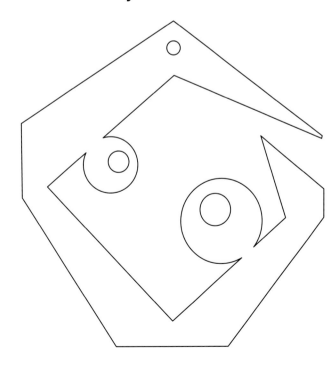

Lucky Star

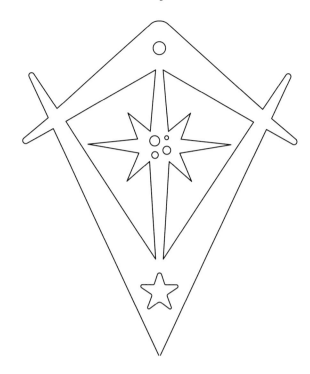

Vintage TV

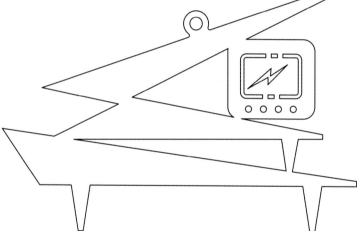

Dazzling Spheres

Cubic Stars

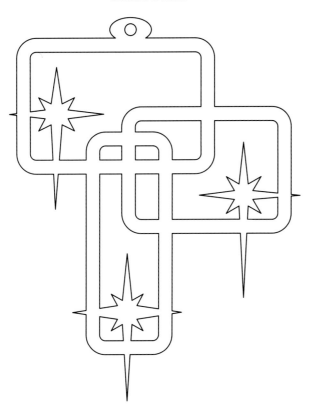

Blazing Star

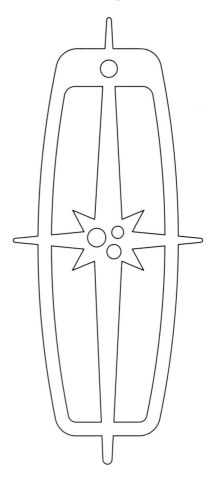

Cubic Finial

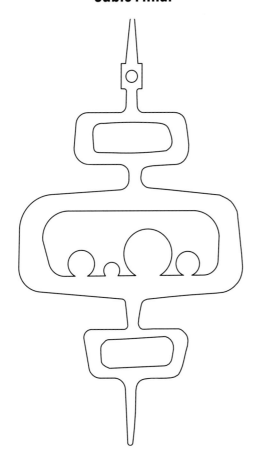

Antique

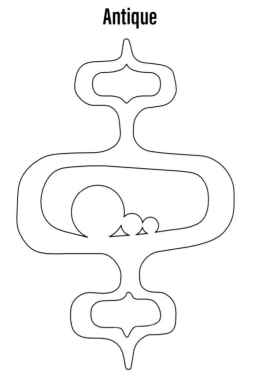

Molecule Prism

New Millennium

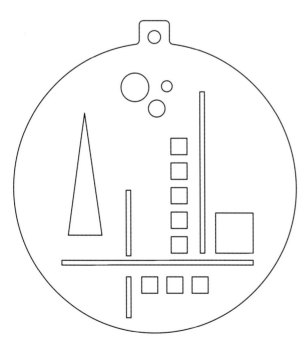

Oval Orbit

Floral Pendant

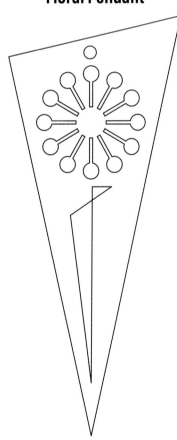

Pyramid of Stars

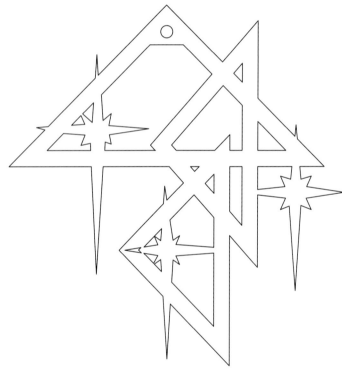

Geometric Cluster

Reaching for the Stars

Sparkly Diamond

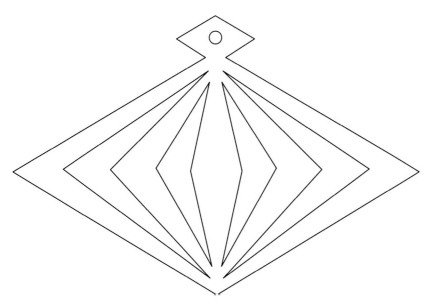

The Magic of Television

Space Needle

Light the Way

Crescent Moon and Stars

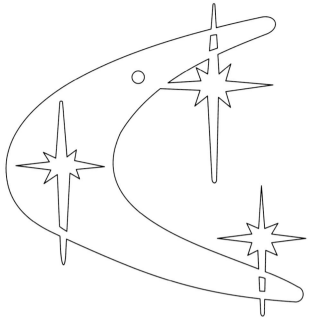

Arctic Waters

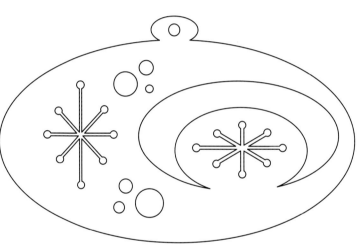

Mid-Century Jewels

Tiki Man

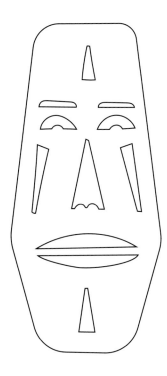

Celestial Bauble

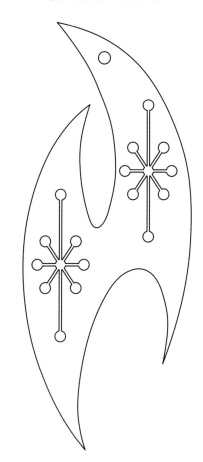

Trio of Abstract Snowflakes

Futuristic Snowflake

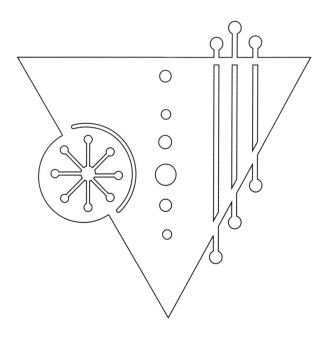

Snowflake Marvel

Linear Sun

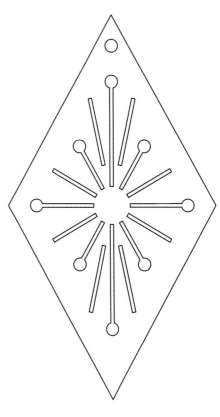

Paperfolding

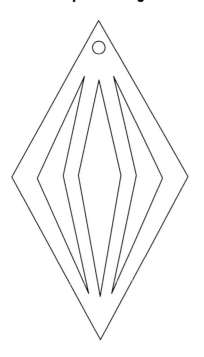

Shining Gemstone

Cosmic Diamonds

Christmas Prism

Shimmering Jewel

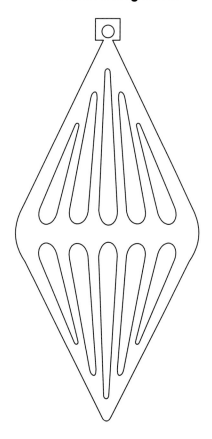

Pair of Bright Stars

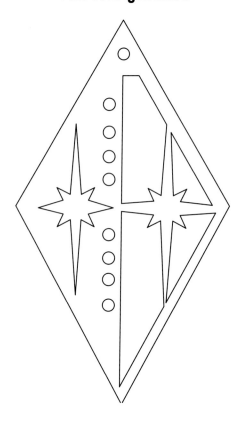

Daylight

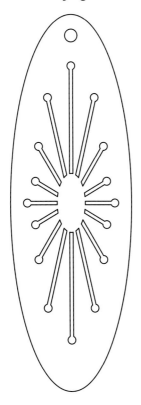

Diverse Triangles

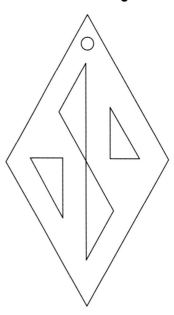

Nordic Easter Egg

Bright as a Diamond

Christmas Star

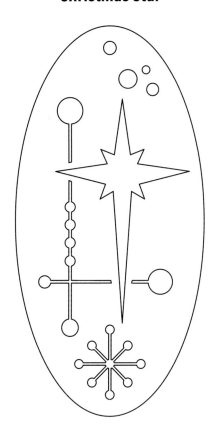

Nordic-Style Flowers

Iconic Christmas Bulbs

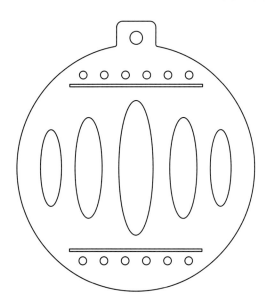

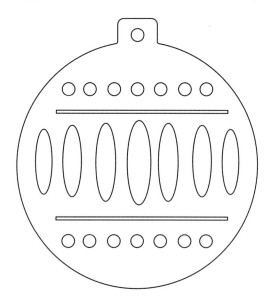

Swimming Minnows

Reflecting Light

High Noon

Row of Diamonds

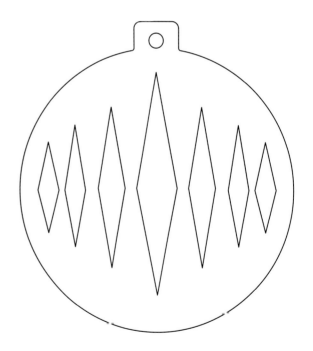

Sunshine and Snow

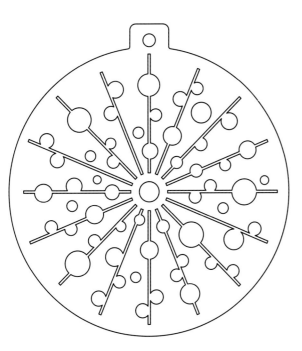

Flying Saucers

Eight-Point Starburst

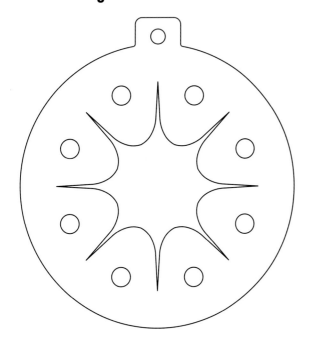

Picasso-Style Bauble

Slivers

Stylish Molecule

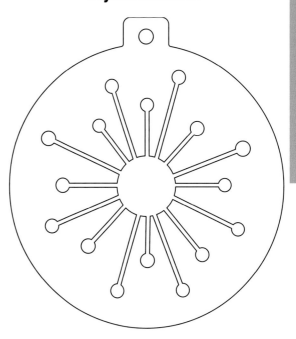

Argyle Sweater

Retro Flower

Classic Bulb

Three Molecules

Shimmering Stars

Interlocking Circles

Winter Storm

Geometric Burst

Dynamic Globe

Hidden Jewels

Modern Starbursts

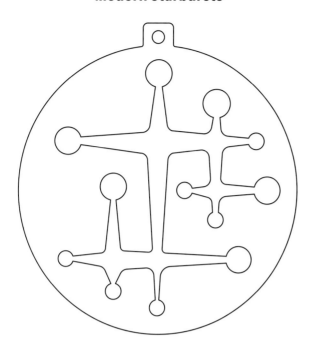

Stars and Stripes

Fizzing Bubbles

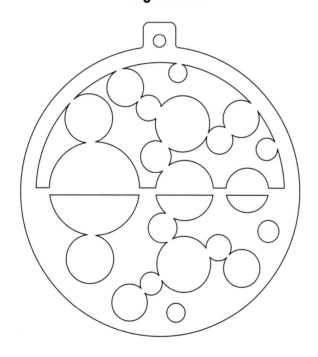

Trio of Ripples

Computer Circuit

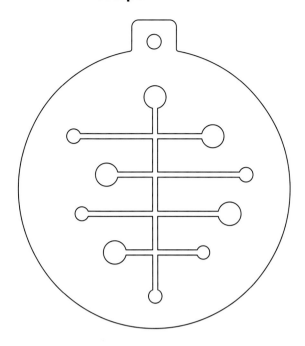

Heavy Snowfall

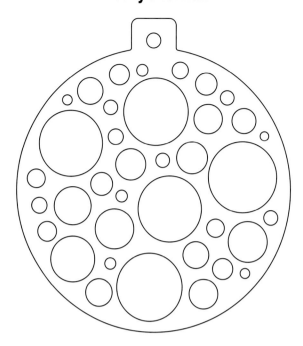

Crescent Spheres

Vintage Snowflakes

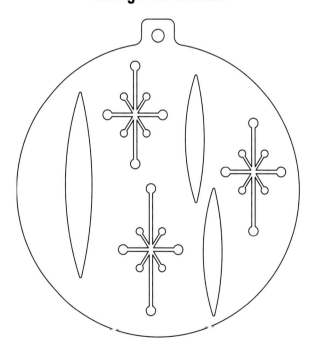

Cubic Trinity

Bursting Bubbles

Quiet Forest

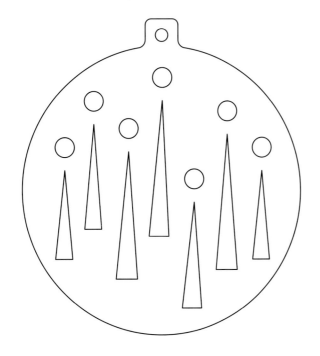

April Showers

Sun Rays

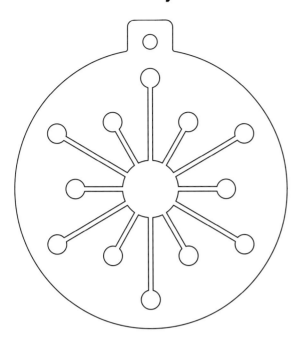

Shining Diamonds

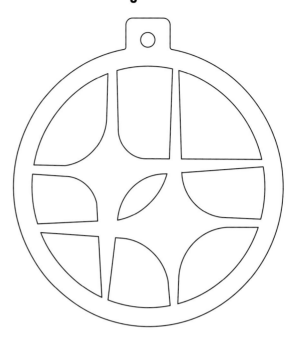

Cosmic Highway

Holiday Maze

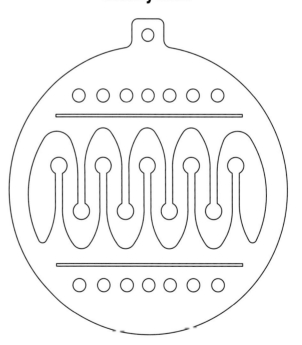

Modern Sunset

Shooting Stars

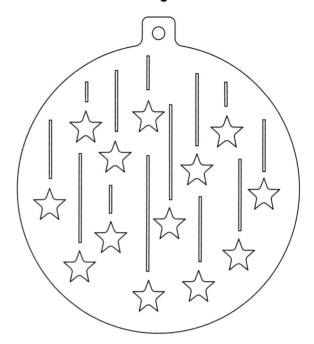

Abstract Mountains

Big Skies

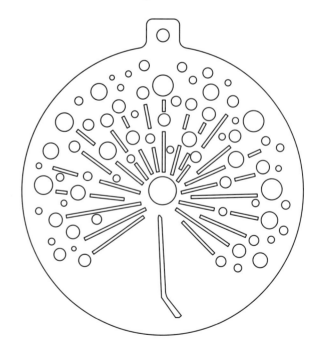

Icicle Bunch

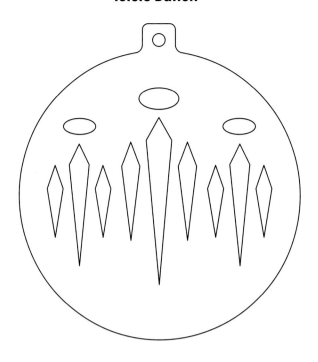

Boomerangs

Flowing Circuits

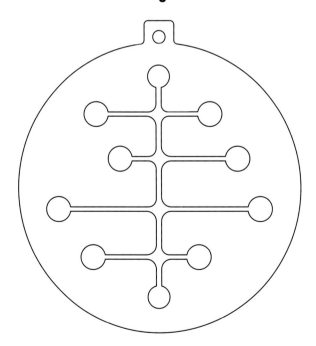

Diamond Bunch

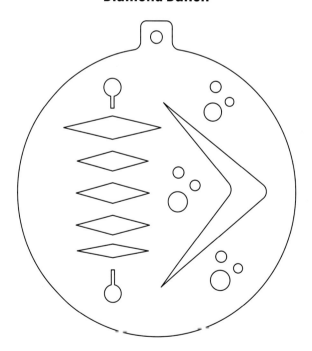

Trio of Diamonds

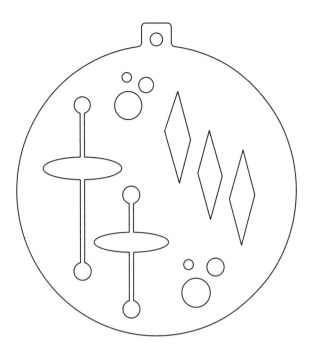

Diamond Trinity

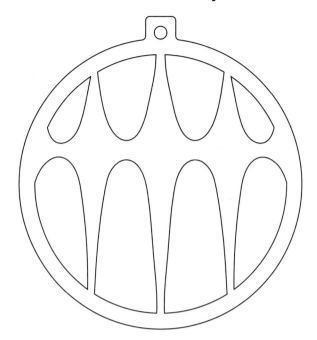

Cluster of Squares

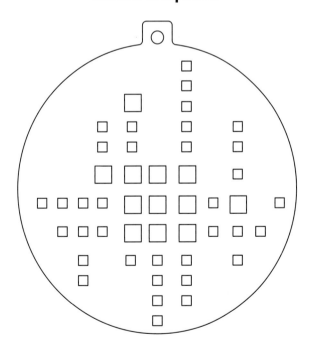

Moongazing

Pair of Diamonds

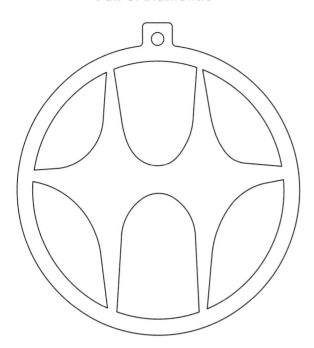

Abstract Tree Roots

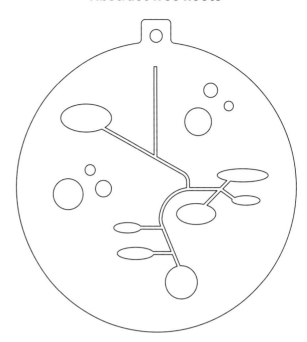

All About Lighting

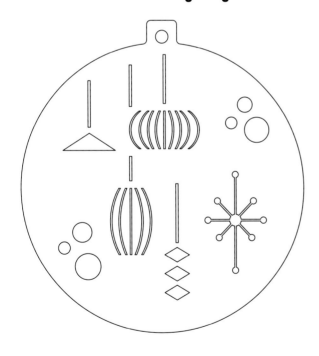

Meteor Shower

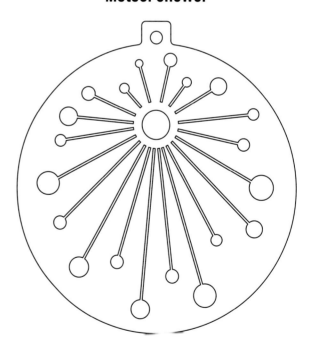

Cheer Up

Circuit Cluster

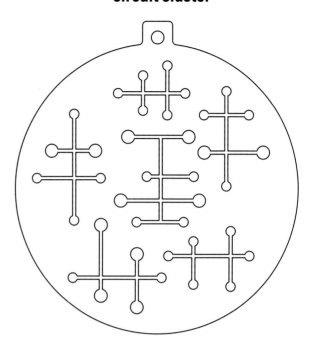

Winter Circuit

Rising Sun

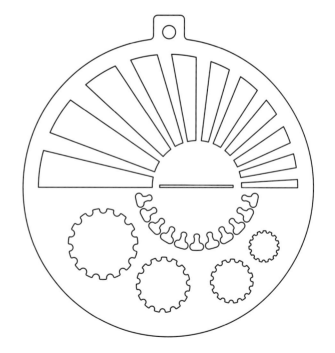

Abstract Obstacle Course

Wonders of Space

Bubble Sun

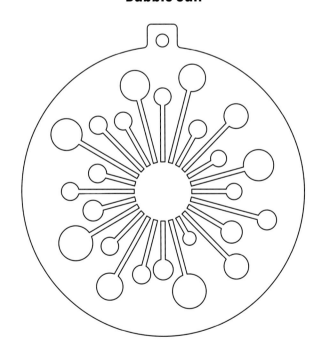

Windmills

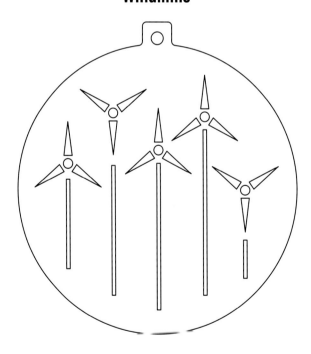

Trio of Boomerangs

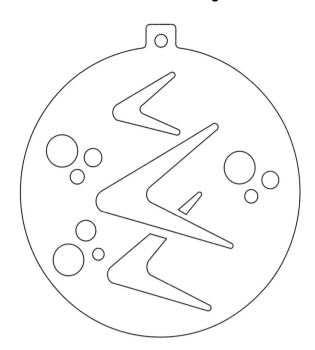

Poinsettia Bauble

Wintry Diamonds

Abstract Burst

Snowflakes and Spirals

Modern Stars

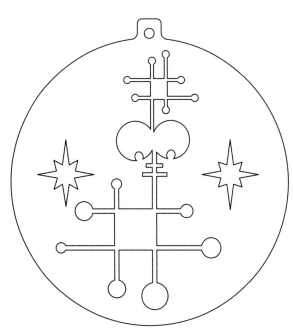

Mid-Century Stars

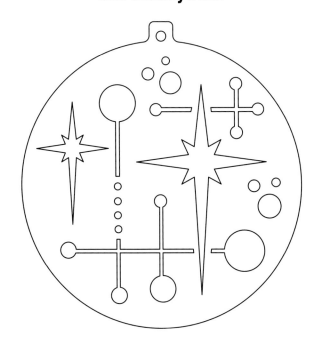

Christmas Night

Geometric Obstacle Course

Bubbly Fun

Driving Through the City

Classic Poinsettia

Topography

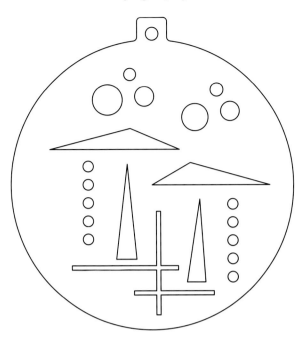

Ski Ramp

Winking Stars

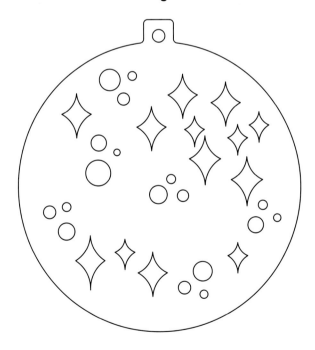

Geometric Slopes

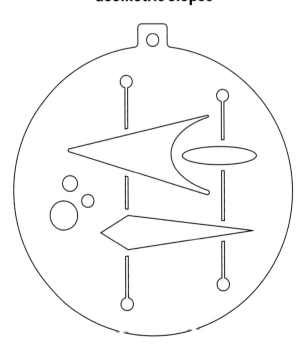

Joy, Love, Peace

Love

Live, Laugh, Love

You Light Up My Life

Read Something New Today

Home Sweet Home

Bowl the Lanes

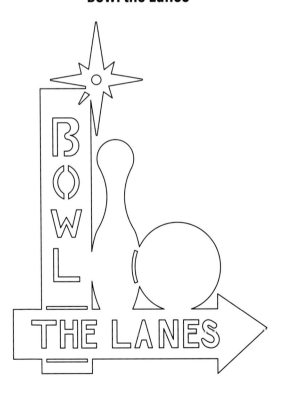

Drive-In

Love and Hearts

Never Never Never Give Up

Bee Yourself

Bee Happy

Peace Sign

Index

A
acrylics and plastics, 9
adhesive removers, 10
Animals
  Aquarium Life, 80
  Bee Mine, 84
  Birds of Prey, 82
  Buzzing Around, 83
  Cat on the Windowsill, 79
  Early Bird, 81
  Elegant Cat, 81
  Equestrian Love, 83
  Festive Feline, 78
  Flock of Flamingoes, 83
  Flying High, 81
  Furry Lookout, 79
  It's a Hoot, 82
  Kitty Cat, 78
  Lion Pride, 84
  Man's Best Friend, 84
  Night Owl, 82
  Nocturnal Pets, 78
  Plenty of Fish, 80
  Purr-fect Place, 79
  Scales and Fins, 82
  School of Fish, 81
  Sharing a Perch, 83
  Something's Fishy, 79
  Squirreling Away, 84
  Swimming Along, 80
  Trio of Kittens, 78
  Under the Sea, 80
Automotive
  Classic Cadillac, 90
  Drag Racing, 91
  Family Vacation, 92
  Futuristic Camper, 94
  Heading to the Beach, 91
  Motorcycle, 95
  Nostalgic Camper, 94
  On the Road, 92
  Out for a Drive, 92
  Propeller Plane, 95
  Retro Trailer, 93
  Retro Truck, 90
  Steam Locomotive, 95
  Speed Racer, 93
  Sunday Drive, 91
  Tractor, 95
  Vacation Motor Home, 94
  Vintage Car, 90
  Vintage Racecar, 93

C
cardstock, 8
carnauba wax, 9
cherry, 8
clear finishes, 9

D
Danish oil, 9

digital cutting machines, 6
displaying, 9

F
fabrics, 8
finishing and displaying, 9
Fun in the Sun
  Hang Ten, 77
  Happy Hour, 75
  It's Five O'Clock
    Somewhere, 76
  Margarita on the Beach, 75
  Martini Time, 76
  Mixing Drinks, 76
  Party, 75
  R&R, 77
  Sunny Day, 75
  Surf's Up, 76
  Tropical Paradise, 77
  Wine Down, 77

H
Hearts and Flowers
  A Single Rose, 73
  An Imprint on Your Heart, 67
  Be My Valentine, 68
  Blooming Iris, 74
  Dandelion Daze, 74
  Delicate Daisy, 70
  Delightful Dandelions, 73
  Duo of Hearts, 67
  Floral Bouquet, 70
  Floral Quilt Block, 70
  Floral Trinity, 73
  Flower Power, 69
  Fresh Lily, 5, 72
  Growing Up, 74
  Heartbeat, 68
  In Full Bloom, 72
  Lovebirds, 68
  Night Garden, 71
  Perfect Petals, 71
  Poinsettia in Bloom, 71
  Spring Awakening, 72
  Spring Blossom, 71
  Star-crossed Lovers, 69
  Sunflowers, 72
  Two Turtle Doves, 69
  Wholesome Love, 5, 67
  Wildflower, 70
Hobbies
  All That Jazz, 87
  Calm Waters, 89
  Cycling, 86
  Gone Fishing, 87
  Hitting the Slopes, 86
  Hoisting the Sails, 87
  Moonlight Sail, 89
  Music Lover, 85
  Nautical Fun, 88

  Out on the Water, 88
  Palm Springs, 85
  Sailing Away, 87
  Sailing the High Seas, 88
  Shooting Hoops, 86
  Soccer, 89
  To a Tee, 85
  Triathlon, 86
Holiday Season
  Abstract Holiday, 18
  Abstract Santa, 33
  Angled Angel, 31
  Beachy Holiday, 20
  Bubble Tree, 32
  Bubbly Christmas Tree, 17
  Celestial Christmas, 23
  Cheerful Santa, 34
  Christmas Bulbs and
    Lights, 33
  Christmas Camping, 39
  Christmas Cheer, 15
  Christmas Love, 27
  Christmas Tree Baubles, 25
  Christmas Tree Baubles
    2, 25
  Christmas Tree Farm, 38
  Christmas Tree Lighting,
    19
  Christmas Tree Lot, 12
  Christmas Vacation, 39
  Dazzling Decorations, 29
  Decorating the Tree, 19
  Delicate Snowflakes, 11
  Diamond Puzzle Tree, 28
  Diamonds and Snowflakes,
    41
  Doe and Fawn, 17
  Elegant Christmas Tree, 11
  Father Christmas, 34
  Festive Douglas Fir, 32
  Festive Finial, 42
  Festive Kris Kringle, 32
  Festive Lights, 36
  Festive Reindeer, 12
  Festive Wreath, 32
  Forest Gathering, 20
  Geometric Christmas Tree
    and Stars, 11
  Geometric Jumble Tree, 27
  Geometric Nativity, 23
  Geometric Santa, 36
  Geometric Snow Tree, 21
  Geometric Star Tree, 22
  Gingerbread Tree, 28
  Guardian Angels, 24
  Happy Hanukkah, 43
  Happy New Year!, 43
  Hark the Angels, 23
  Heralding Angel, 37
  Holiday Joy, 29

  Holiday Travels, 38
  Holy Church, 24
  In the Manger, 37
  Jolly St. Nick, 10, 33
  Kris Kringle in a Box, 35
  Leaping Reindeer, 16
  Let it Snow, 16
  Light in the East, 13
  Majestic Reindeer, 16
  Merry Christmas, 14
  Mid-Century Modern
    Christmas, 19
  Mid-Century Reindeer, 30
  Mid-Century Snowflakes,
    41
  Miniature Trees, 21
  Modern Holiday, 25
  Modern Santa, 31
  Modern Teardrop Swirl, 42
  Moonlit Church, 24
  Nativity, 22
  New Year Celebrations, 40
  North Star, 43
  Nutcracker, 30
  O' Holy Night, 40
  Oblong Tree, 27
  Patterned Pines, 18
  Patterned Tree, 26
  Peace & Unity, 15
  Peace on Earth, 15
  Peaceful Drive, 5, 39
  Picking Out the Family
    Tree, 38
  Presents Under the Tree,
    36
  Reindeer Duo, 17
  Reindeer Joy, 18
  Retro Holiday, 28
  Santa and Snowflakes, 14
  Santa Delivering Presents,
    35
  Secluded Sapling, 40
  Snowfall, 13
  Snowflake Christmas
    Tree, 20
  Snowflake Puzzle Tree, 21
  Snowflake Teardrop Swirl,
    42
  Snowy Reindeer, 22
  Spiny Tree, 27
  Spiral Tree, 29
  Squares Christmas Tree, 11
  Starburst, 26
  Starry Forest, 17
  Starry Love, 4, 15
  Starry Nativity, 23
  Starry Night, 12
  Starry Puzzle Trees, 22
  Starry Tree and Snowflake,
    18

  Starry Tree Delight, 21
  String up the Lights, 28
  Stylish Diamond, 19
  Stylish Snowflakes, 41
  Teardrop Christmas Tree,
    31
  Teardrop Snowflake, 31
  Tinsel and Lights, 20
  Toy Soldier, 29
  Traditional Snowflake, 34
  Trimming the Tree, 13
  Trinity, 25
  Trio of Trees, 35
  Tumbling Triangles Tree,
    26
  Twinkling Stars, 16
  Under the Tree, 13
  Winter Cross, 37
  Winter Love, 14
  Winter Peace, 14
  Wooded Church, 245

L
laser cutters, 6

M
maple, 8
materials, choosing, 8-9
metal, thin, 9
Miscellaneous Shapes and
  Objects
  Abstract Bowtie, 109
  Abstract Burst, 142
  Abstract Mountains, 136
  Abstract Obstacle Course,
    141
  Abstract Pendant, 110
  Abstract Tree Roots, 139
  Abstract Trinket, 105
  All About Lighting, 139
  Antique, 117
  April Showers, 134
  Arctic Waters, 121
  Argyle Sweater, 129
  Atom Molecule, 107
  Atomic Snowflake, 106
  Big Skies, 136
  Blazing Star, 116
  Blowing Bubbles, 111
  Boomerangs, 137
  Bright as a Diamond, 125
  Bubble Sun, 141
  Bubble Trouble, 108
  Bubbly Explosion, 110
  Bubbly Fun, 144
  Bursting Bubbles, 134
  Cat-Eye Sunglasses, 105
  Celestial Bauble, 122
  Celestial Finial, 109
  Cheer Up, 140
  Cheese and Olives, 109

Christmas Memories, 107
Christmas Night, 143
Christmas Prism, 124
Christmas Star, 126
Circuit Cluster, 140
Classic Bulb, 130
Classic Poinsettia, 144
Cluster of Squares, 138
Computer Circuit, 133
Cosmic Diamonds, 124
Cosmic Highway, 135
Crescent Moon and Stars, 121
Crescent Spheres, 133
Cubic Finial, 116
Cubic Stars, 116
Cubic Trinity, 134
Daylight, 125
Dazzling Spheres, 115
Diamond Bunch, 137
Diamond Trinity, 138
Diverse Triangles, 125
Driving Through the City, 144
Dynamic Globe, 131
Dynamic Swirl, 114
Eight-Point Starburst, 128
Expanding Bulb, 111
Fizzing Bubbles, 132
Floating Bubbles, 112
Floral Pendant, 118
Flowing Circuits, 137
Flying Saucers, 128
Forest Silhouette, 113
Futuristic Finial, 103
Futuristic Snowflake, 122
Geometric Burst, 131
Geometric Cluster, 119
Geometric Diamond, 112
Geometric Obstacles Course, 144
Geometric Slopes, 145
Groovy Lava Lamp, 106
Heavy Snowfall, 133
Hidden Jewels, 131
High Noon, 127
Holiday Maze, 135
Icicle Bunch, 137
Iconic Christmas Bulbs, 126
Interlocking Circles, 130
Light the Way, 120
Linear Sun, 123
Looking Out the Window, 107
Lucky Star, 115
Lunar Bauble, 106
Magic of Television, The, 120
Melting Bauble, 108
Mesopotamian Bulb, 108
Meteor Shower, 139
Mid-Century Bauble, 109

Mid-Century Jewels, 121
Mid-Century Stars, 143
Modern Starbursts, 132
Modern Stars, 143
Modern Sunset, 136
Modern Triangle, 105
Modern Windowsills, 112
Molecule Prism, 117
Moon and Stars, 113
Moongazing, 138
Mountain Peak, 113
New Millennium, 117
Nordic Easter Egg, 125
Nordic-Style Flowers, 126
Oval Orbit, 118
Pair of Bright Stars, 124
Pair of Diamonds, 139
Pair of Snowflakes, 111
Paperfolding, 123
Picasso-Style Bauble, 128
Poinsettia Bauble, 142
Pyramid of Stars, 118
Quiet Forest 134
Reaching for the Stars, 119
Reflecting Light, 127
Retro Flower, 129
Retro Radio, 104
Retro Television, 106
Rising Sun, 140
Row of Diamonds, 127
Slivers, 129
Shimmering Jewel, 124
Shimmering Stars, 130
Shining Diamonds, 135
Shining Gemstone, 123
Shooting Stars, 136
Ski Ramp, 145
Snowflakes and Spirals, 143
Snowflake Marvel, 123
Solar Power, 111
Space Needle, 120
Sparkly Diamond, 119
Stacked Ovals, 114
Stack of Olives, 110
Stars and Stripes. 132
Striped Snowflake, 107
Stylish Molecule, 129
Sun Rays, 135
Sunburst 105
Sunshine and Snow, 128
Swimming Minnows, 127
Three Molecules, 130
Tiki Man, 122
Topography, 145
Trio of Abstract Snowflakes, 122
Trio of Boomerangs, 142
Trio of Diamonds, 138
Trio of Ripples, 132
Vintage Alarm Clock, 104
Vintage Snowflakes 133
Vintage TV, 115

Windmills, 141
Winking Stars, 145
Winter Circuit, 140
Winter Magic, 114
Winter Storm, 131
Wintry Diamonds, 142
Wonders of Space, 141
Mixing Drinks, 76
Modern Holiday, 25
Modern Icicle, 51
Modern Santa, 31
Modern Starbursts, 132
Modern Stars, 143
Modern Sunset, 136
Modern Teardrop Swirl, 42
Modern Triangle, 105
Modern Windowsills, 112
Molecule Prism, 117
Moon and Stars, 113
Moongazing, 138
Moonlight Sail, 89
Moonlit Church, 24
Motorcycle, 95
Mountain Peak, 113
Music Lover, 85

N
natural finishes, 9
P
paints, 9
paper, 8
patterns, 10-149
plastics, 9
plywood, 8
protect your lungs, 7

S
safety, 7
Science Fiction
Alien Ship, 96
Android Head, 103
Antique Lantern, 104
Blast Off!, 99
Cosmic Bot, 103
Cruising Through the Stars, 102
Futuristic City, 102
Futuristic Droid, 10, 100
In Orbit, 101
Jukebox, 103
Out of This World, 102
Outer Space, 97
Robot, 100
Rocket, 99
Sci-Fi Television, 98
Space Landing, 97
Space Launch, 98
Space Odyssey, 101
Space Travel, 98
Spacecraft, 97
Spaceship, 96
Starship, 99

Traveling through Space and Time, 101
UFO, 100
Ultramodern City Finial, 102
Utopian Metropolis, 96
scroll saws, 6
stains, 9
Stars
Astral Collection, 66
Celestial Trio, 5, 64
Cluster of Stars, 65
Cosmic Delight, 63
Elegant Luminary, 65
Interstellar, 65
Rising Star, 66
Star Bright, 62
Stardust, 63
Starlight, 65
Stellar Light, 64
Stylish Galaxy, 66
Supernova, 64
Superstar, 62
Trinity of Stars, 63
Winter Nebula, 62

T
thin metal, 9
tools, 6
V
vinyl, 8
W
walnut, 8
washes, 9
Winter
Abstract Forest, 47
Abstract Icicle, 51
Alpine Icicle, 58
Arctic Knitwear, 60
Arctic Morning, 54
Argyle Snowflake Finial, 57
Argyle Winter, 45
Black Diamond Run, 57
Bubble Snowflake, 49
Bubbly Snowflake, 46
Bundled Up Frosty, 49
Bustling Blizzard, 48
Chilly Nights, 56
Chilly Winds, 54
Cozy Sweater Finial, 57
Diamond Snowflake, 50
Elegant Snowflake, 46
Flurry Fun, 55
Following the Star, 61
Freezing Cold, 53
Frosty Trinket, 54
Futuristic Icicle, 52
Geometric Icicle, 51
Geometric Snowman, 50
Geometric Storm, 45
Graceful Snowflakes, 55
Hailstorm, 60
Happy Snowman, 48

Holiday Bow, 59
Ice Storm, 56
Jingle Bells, 61
Light Up the Night Sky, 49
Lovely Poinsettia, 50
Melting Icicle, 59
Mid-Century Icicle, 52
Mid-Century Winter, 44
Modern Icicle, 51
Nighttime Snowfall, 61
Nordic Spiral, 58
Nordic Touch, 48
Northern Lights, 49
Peppermint Swirl, 56
Scandinavian Bauble, 10, 60
Seasonal Flurry, 53
Seasonal Pine Needles, 47
Serene Forest, 46
Snow Angels, 61
Snow Day, 55
Snowball Fight, 55
Snowball Finial, 53
Snowbird, 56
Snowflake Bauble, 52
Snowflake Finial, 48
Snowflake Season, 44
Snowy Night, 44
Star of Bethlehem, 60
Stargazing, 47
Starry Icicle, 54
Stylish Icicle, 51
Sweater Weather, 46
Tranquil Snowfall, 50
Ultramodern Icicle, 58
Ultramodern Snowflake, 47
Unique Snowflake, 59
Winter Crystal, 59
Winter Fever, 58
Winter Solstice, 44
Winter Wonderland, 45
Wintertime, 57
Wintry Nights, 45
wood, 8
Words
Bee Happy, 149
Bee Yourself, 149
Bowl the Lanes, 147
Drive-In, 148
Home Sweet Home, 147
Joy, Love, Peace, 10, 146
Live, Laugh, Love, 146
Love, 146
Love and Hearts, 148
Never Never Never Give Up, 148
Peace Sign, 149
Read Something New Today, 147
You Light Up My Life, 147

About the Author

Frederick Arndt is a native of Michigan who has had a lifelong interest in the arts and architecture. He earned his bachelor's degree from Kettering University in Flint, Michigan, and his graduate degree from the Sloan School of Business at Stanford University, in Palo Alto, California. Frederick enjoyed a thirty-two-year professional career at General Motors, later Delphi Corporation, where he held various engineering and management positions. In 2005, he retired from Delphi Corporation to turn his love of design into an exciting second career as an artist.

Frederick's portfolio includes a wide range of home décor and artistic designs that are strongly influenced by the shapes and forms of mid-century modern design. His designs are refined, clean, practical, functional, and fun. His work encompasses a wide range of functional and decorative objects, including sculptures, wall art, fretworks, Christmas ornaments, kitchen items, mobiles, static and kinetic art, furniture, room dividers, easels, and more.

Frederick's works also include a distinctive collection of trademarked characters called Modern Eyes in Art™, available as original hand-inked drawings and limited-edition prints. These whimsical creations blend his uniquely stylistic eye designs with iconic shapes to produce art that is both creative and timeless.

Frederick describes his design philosophy as follows: "I have very strong tastes and preferences when it comes to art and home décor design. I have adopted a design philosophy that is simply to create objects that I would want to buy, use, and enjoy but aren't commercially available. I strive for my works to be pleasing to the eye and to combine clean, refined style with practical functionality. I believe form and function must be carefully balanced to achieve outstanding design."

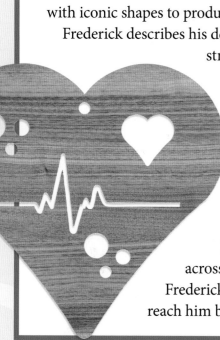

Frederick's artwork is sold through select galleries and studios across the United States and is also available online at his Etsy store, Frederick Arndt Artworks (*www.etsy.com/shop/FredArndtArtworks*). You can reach him by email at *fparndt@aol.com*.